TIMELESS

SIMPLE WEDDING DRESS IDEAS

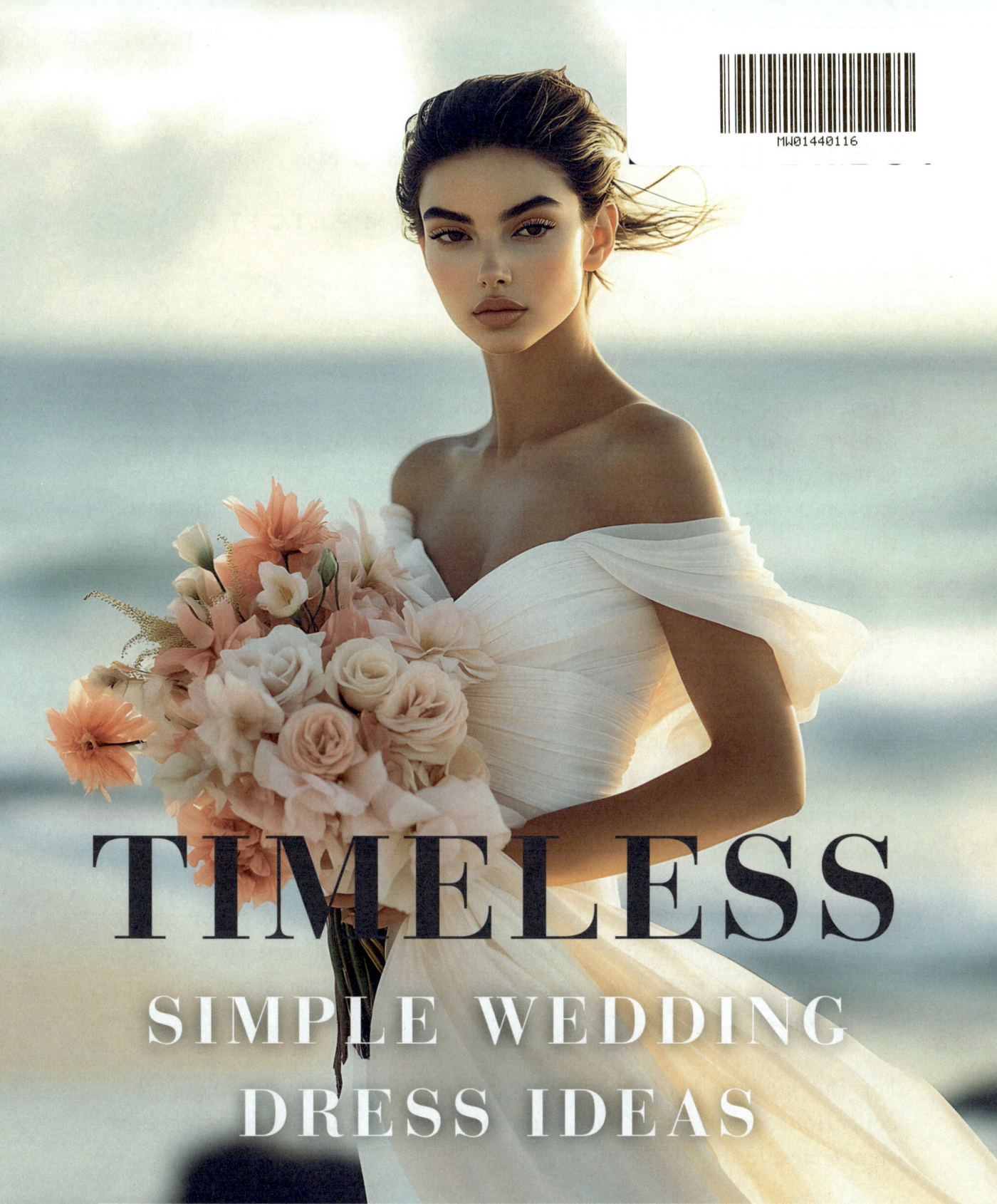

A Fashion and Style Guide to Minimalist, Modern Bridal Gowns.

INTRODUCTION
THE BEAUTY OF SIMPLICITY

In a world where wedding fashion is often synonymous with opulence and grandeur, there is something uniquely striking about a gown that embraces simplicity. Minimalist wedding dresses captivate with their quiet sophistication, allowing the silhouette, the quality of the fabric, and the precision of the tailoring to take center stage.

This book celebrates understated elegance, showcasing refined, modern, and timeless gowns. It is a tribute to brides who seek an effortlessly chic look, proving that a wedding dress does not need excessive embellishments to make a statement. Instead, the true power of a gown lies in its ability to enhance the bride's natural beauty without distraction.

The book explores minimalism and the interpretation of bridal fashion through carefully curated images and thoughtful descriptions. Whether it's a sleek satin slip dress, a structured gown, or a flowing chiffon masterpiece, each dress tells a story of grace and simplicity.

For the modern bride who values sophistication over excess, this collection serves as a source of inspiration and a reminder that sometimes, less truly is more.

TABLE OF CONTENTS

INTRODUCTION

MINIMALIST BRIDAL FASHION — 01

MINIMALIST DRESSES WITH A UNIQUE TWIST — 02

SIMPLE COUTURE GOWNS — 03

EMBELLISHED MINIMALISM — 04

MODERN LACE — 05

CONCLUSION

CHAPTER 1

MINIMALIST BRIDAL FASHION

— 66 ——

Minimalist bridal fashion is not merely a trend; it is a philosophy. It values quality over quantity, precision over extravagance, and refinement over excess. It is an aesthetic that embraces purity of form, allowing the dress to speak through its design rather than through layers of embellishment.

At its core, minimalism in wedding fashion is about intentionality. Every aspect of a minimalist gown, from the choice of fabric to the shape of the neckline, is carefully considered. There are no unnecessary details, no distractions, only a balance of shape, structure, and movement. A minimalist dress does not hide behind lace or beading; instead, it draws attention to the craftsmanship and the bride herself.

This chapter delves into the fundamental elements that define minimalist bridal fashion. It explores how simplicity can be powerful, how clean lines can exude confidence, and how subtle details, such as a well-placed seam or perfectly draped fabric, can elevate a dress to a work of art. Whether inspired by modern architecture, classic tailoring, or effortless elegance, minimalist wedding dresses redefine what it means to be bridal, proving that beauty lies in simplicity.

—————— 99 —

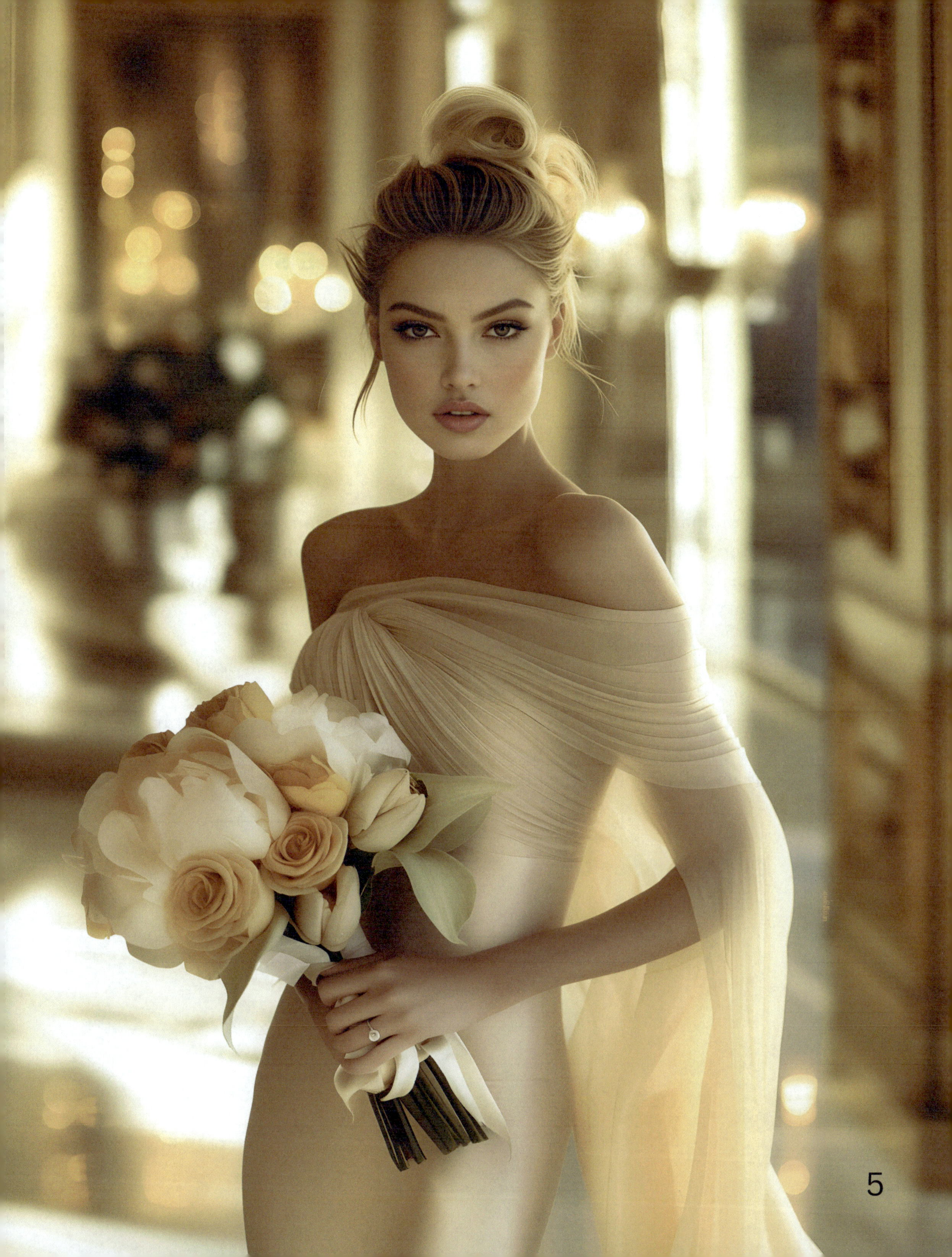

SILHOUETTES & STYLES FOR THE MODERN BRIDE

— 66 ———

The silhouette of a wedding dress is its foundation. In minimalist design, where ornamentation is minimal, the gown's shape takes precedence. The right silhouette can enhance the bride's natural beauty, creating a flattering, effortlessly stylish look.

Each of these silhouettes offers brides a way to embrace simplicity while staying true to their style. Without heavy embellishments, the structure of the dress becomes the star, proving that a well-designed gown needs nothing more than impeccable tailoring to shine.

——— 99 —

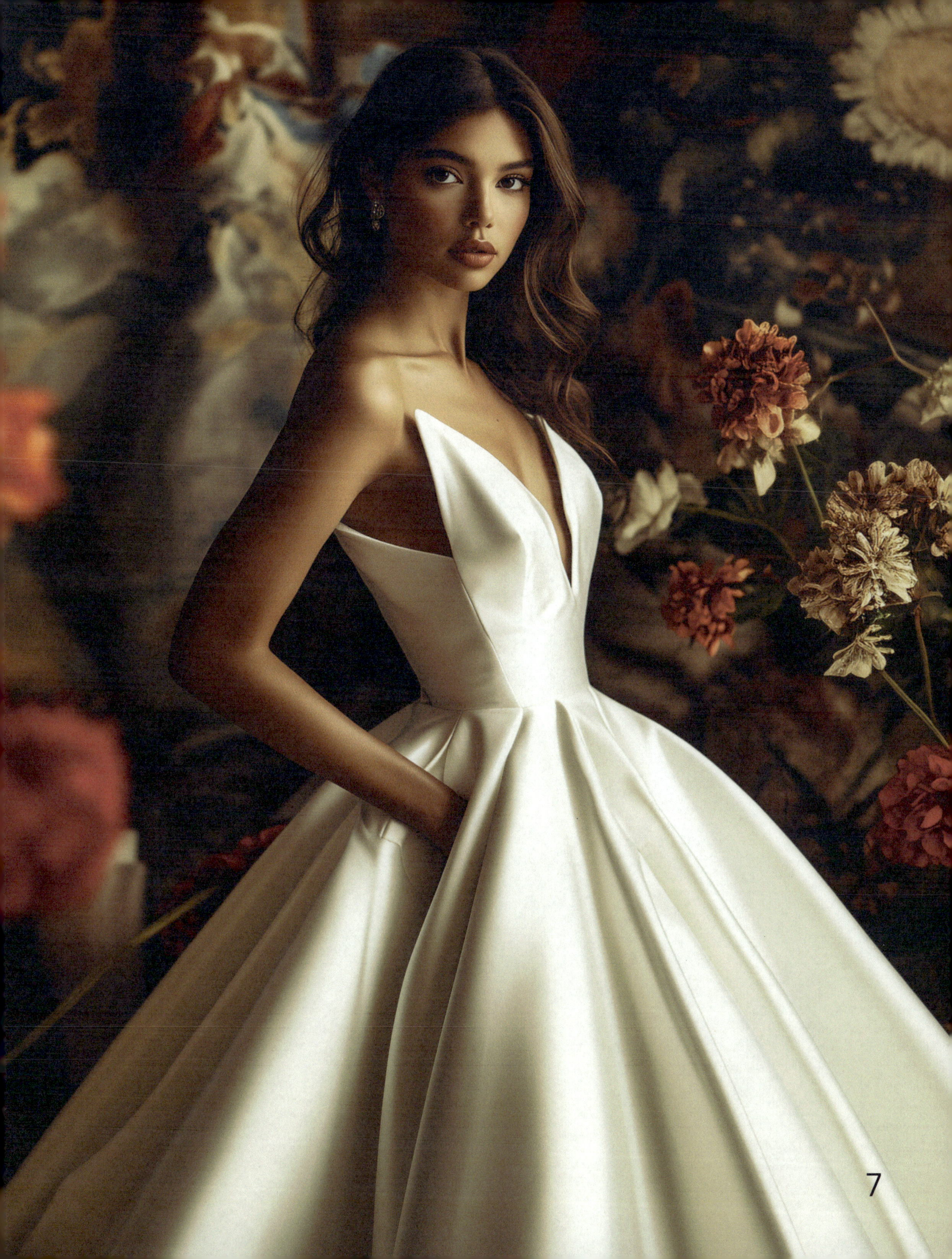

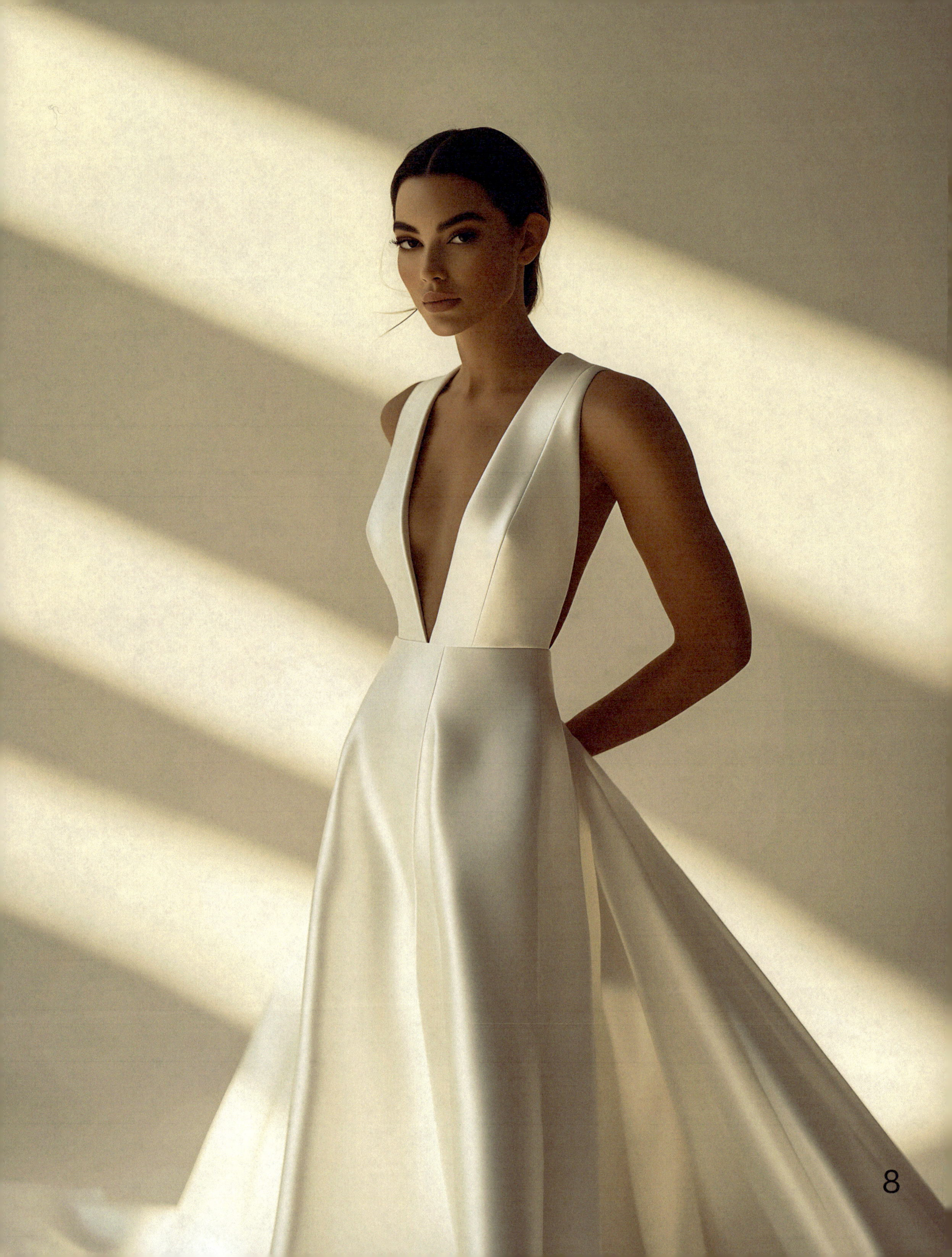

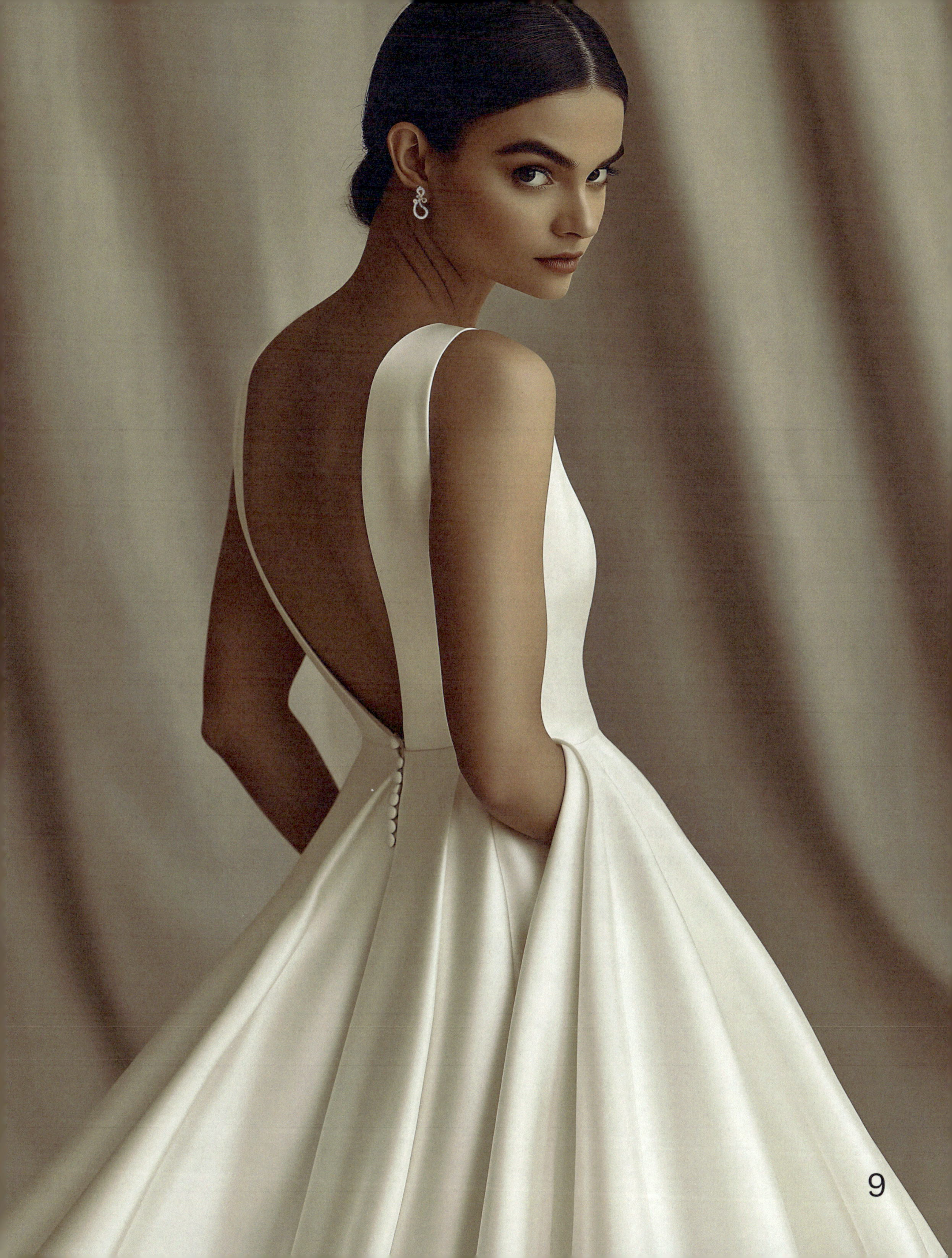

MODERN MINIMALISM

— 66 ———————

In a world where luxury often takes center stage, modern minimalism proves that less can be infinitely more. Brides who embrace this aesthetic appreciate understated elegance, where every detail is intentional. The beauty of any couture gown lies in its precision, silhouette, and luxurious simplicity.

Modern minimalist couture gowns eliminate unnecessary embellishments, emphasizing flawless tailoring, clean lines, and high-quality fabrics. Materials like silk crepe, satin, and structured mikado take precedence, allowing the cut and fit of the gown to take center stage instead of relying on intricate lace or heavy beading.

These dresses often showcase architectural draping, sleek column silhouettes, and plunging or sculptural necklines, making them an ideal choice for the modern bride who values refinement and sophistication.

——————— 99 —

11

SLEEK & CHIC COUTURE GOWNS

> *Modern minimalist gowns embody a quiet confidence and a harmonious blend of boldness and restraint, showcasing elegance from impeccable craftsmanship and effortless beauty rather than excessive details.*
>
> *From silky slip dresses reminiscent of 1990s supermodel fashion to structured gowns with sharp tailoring and striking simplicity, this chapter explores the power of modern couture minimalism. These designs are perfect for brides who appreciate clean aesthetics, contemporary luxury, and timeless style with a modern edge.*

13

14

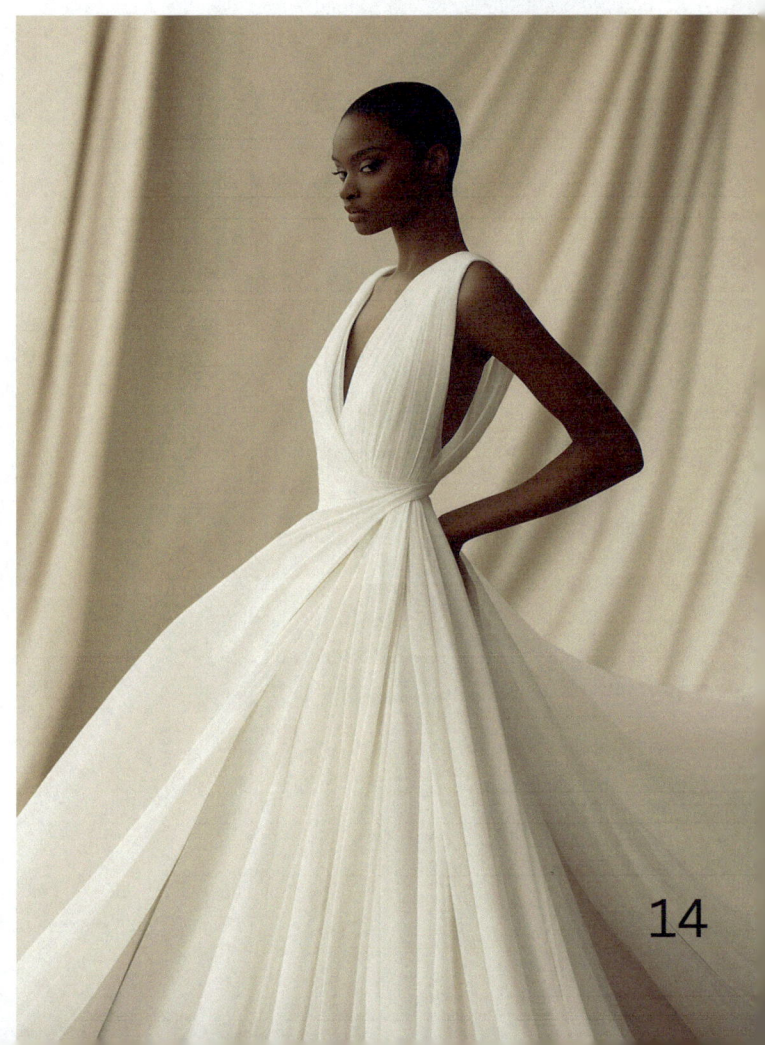

15

16

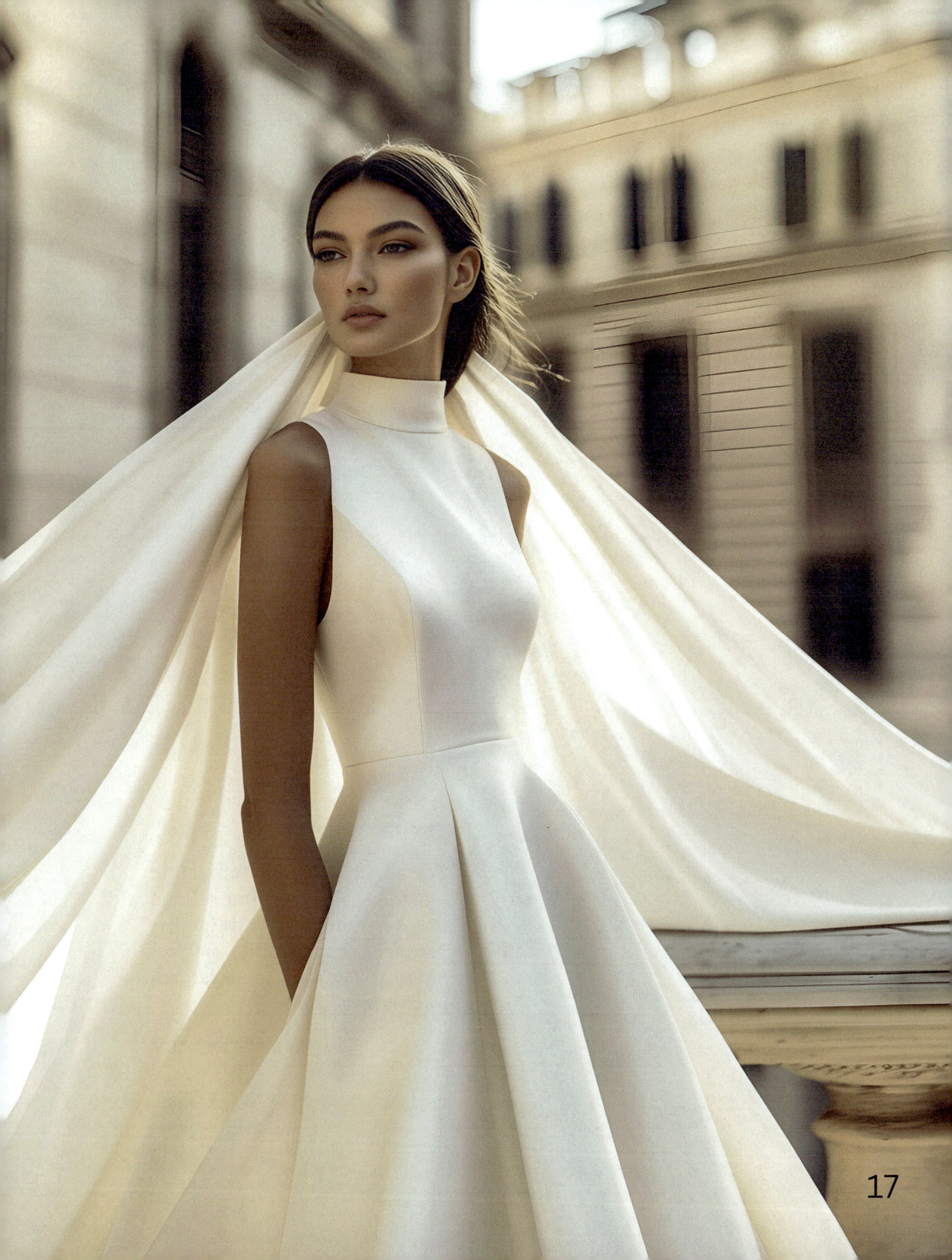

> For brides who appreciate effortless elegance and refined beauty, modern minimalist couture provides the perfect balance between understated and unforgettable.

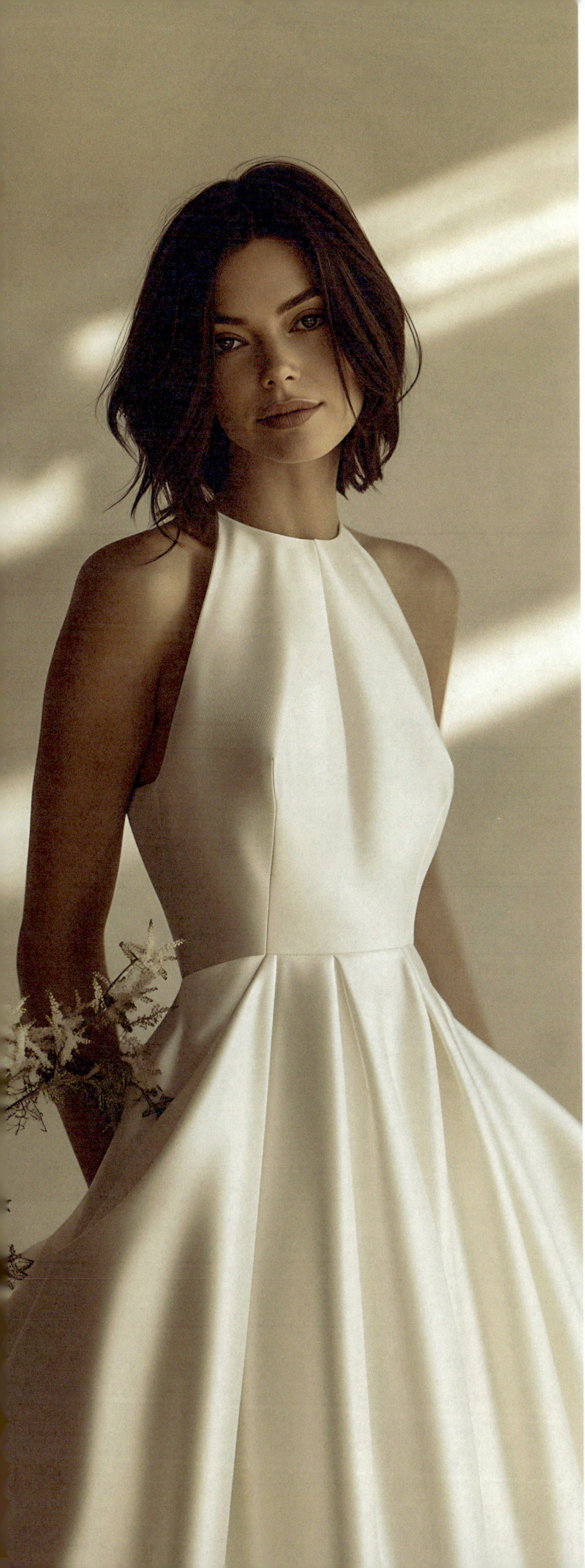
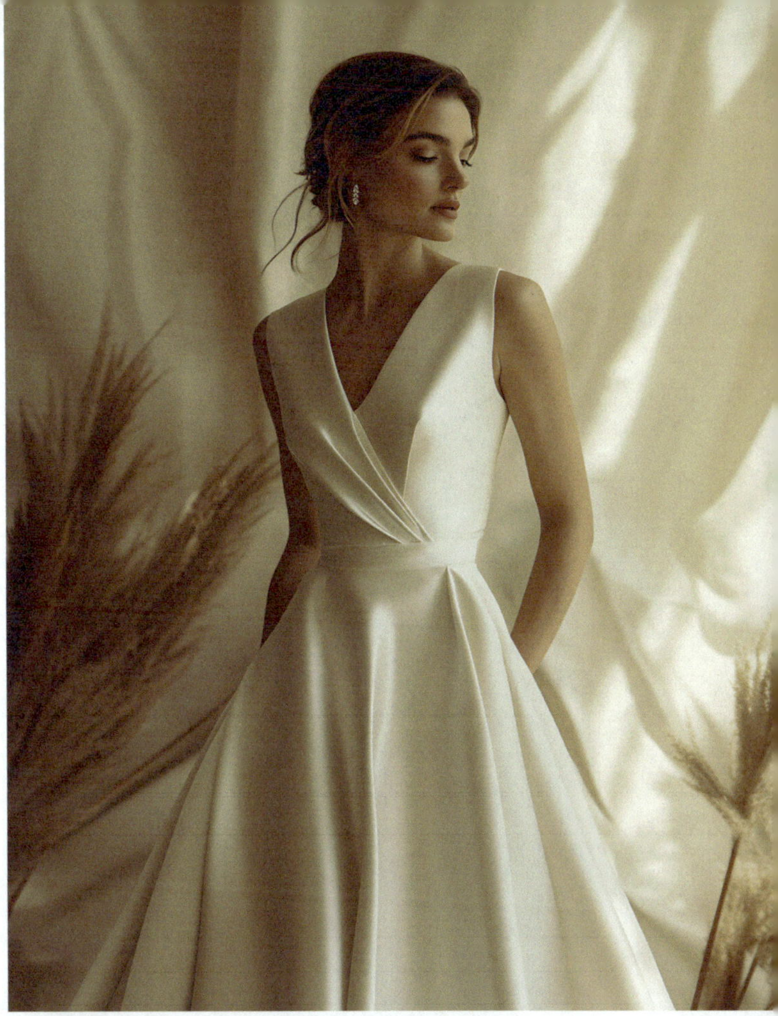
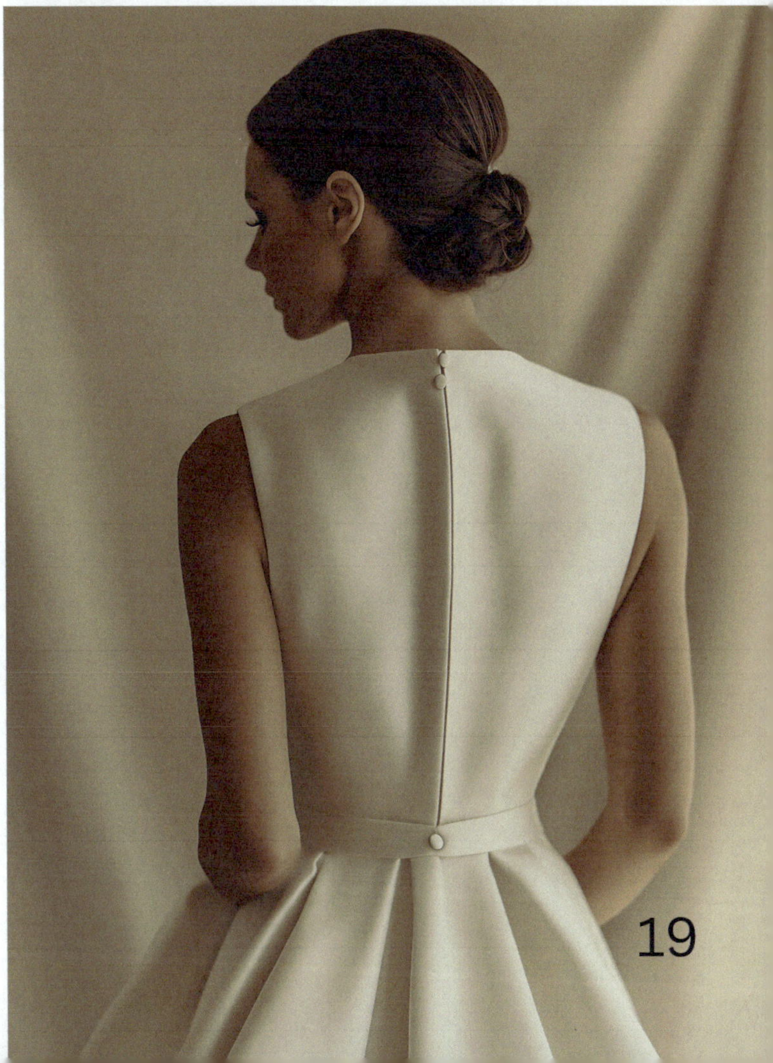

20

— 66 ——————

Some gowns incorporate sleek architectural elements, while others flow gracefully with soft, organic designs, resulting in an elegant yet natural appearance. Inspired by high-fashion runways, contemporary art, and the quiet luxury movement, these gowns are a concept that prioritizes restraint, quality, and timeless appeal over fleeting trends.

Whether featuring a bold asymmetrical neckline, a daringly simple slip dress, or a sharply tailored ensemble, these designs celebrate a less-is-more philosophy that feels refreshingly modern.

—————— 99 —

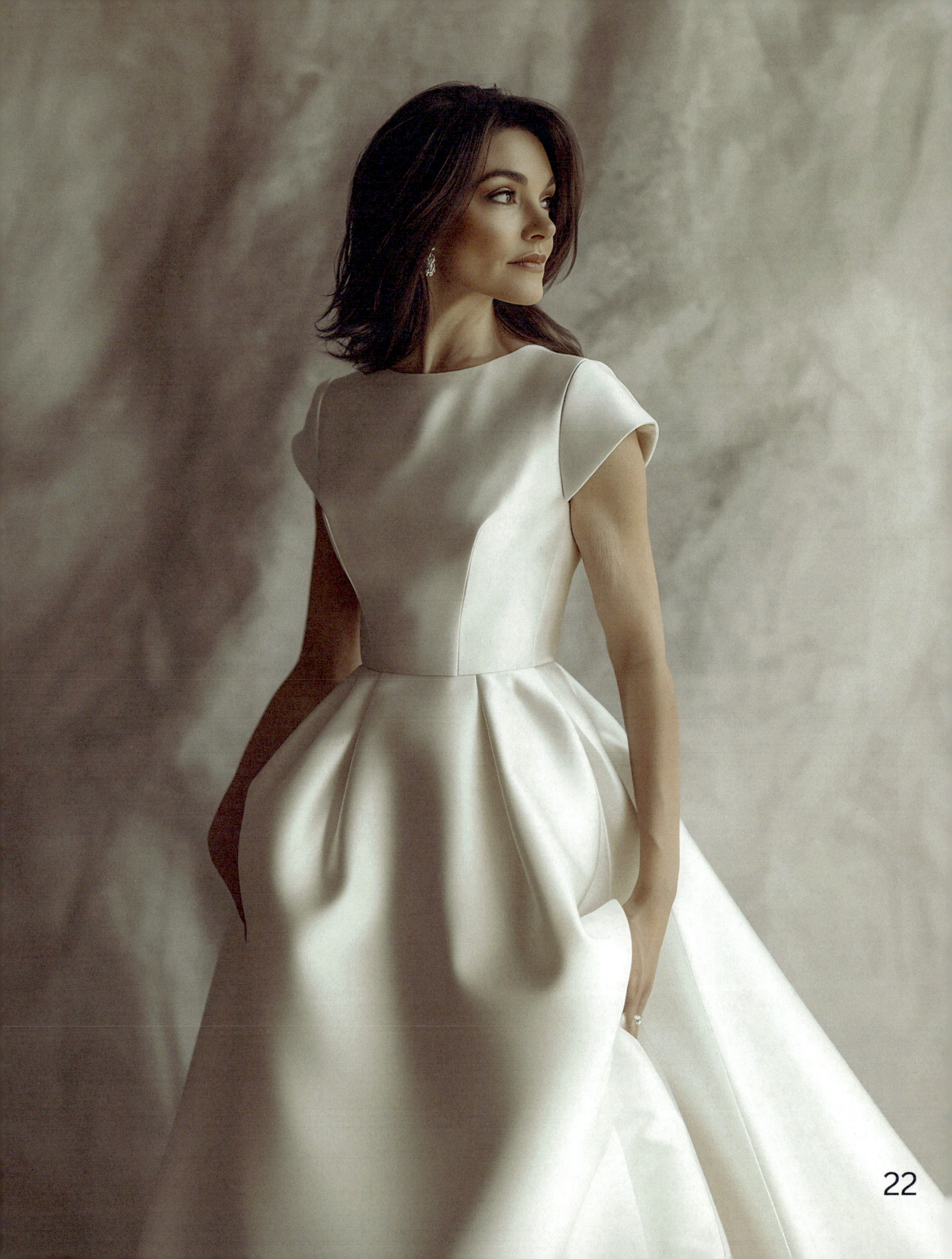

23

24

25

26

27

28

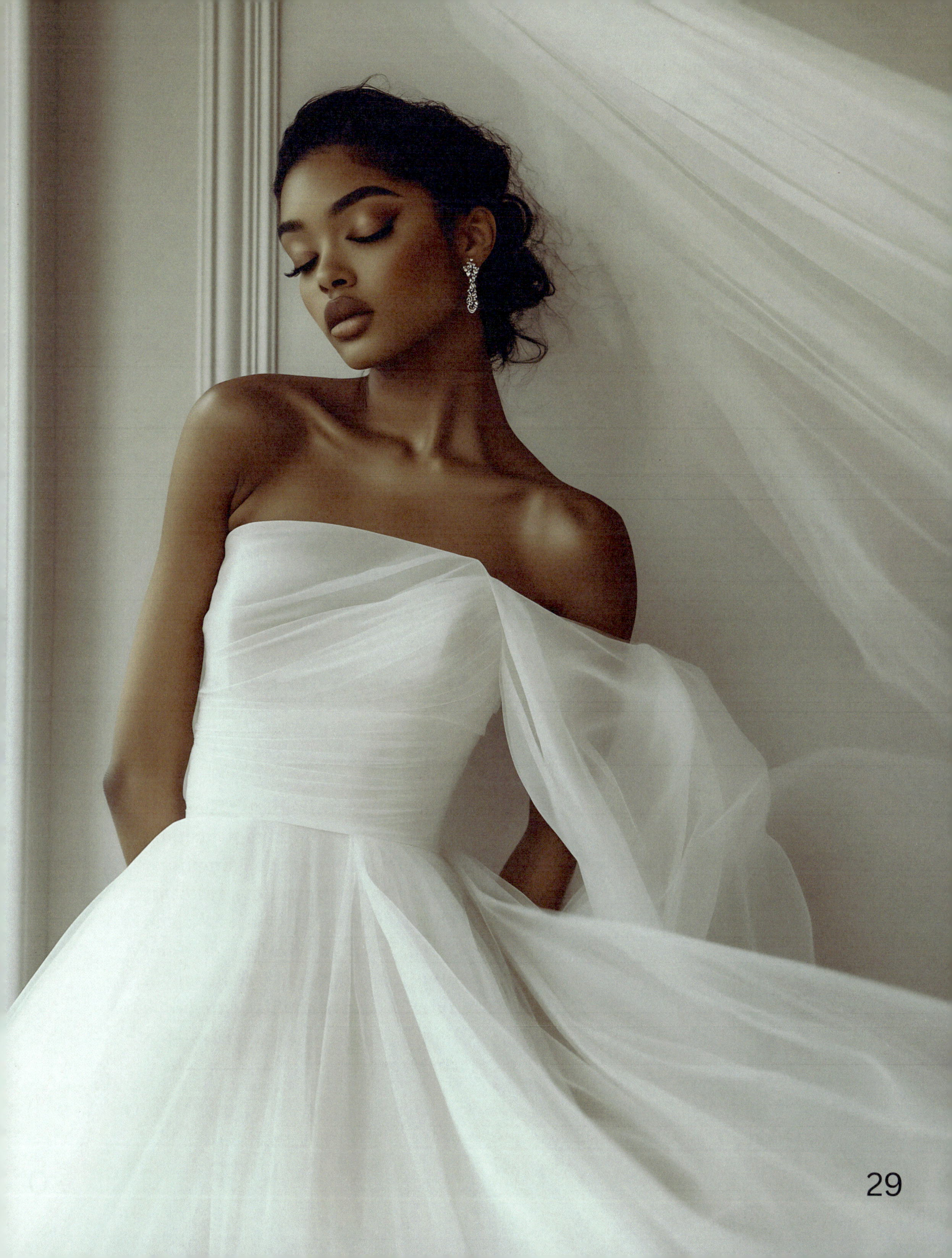

Modern Designs

———— " ————

Modern minimalist couture gowns transform bridal fashion, demonstrating that simplicity can be as impactful as grandeur. These gowns emphasize clean lines, expert tailoring, and luxurious fabrics, resulting in an effortlessly sophisticated look that is both contemporary and timeless.

———————— " —

31

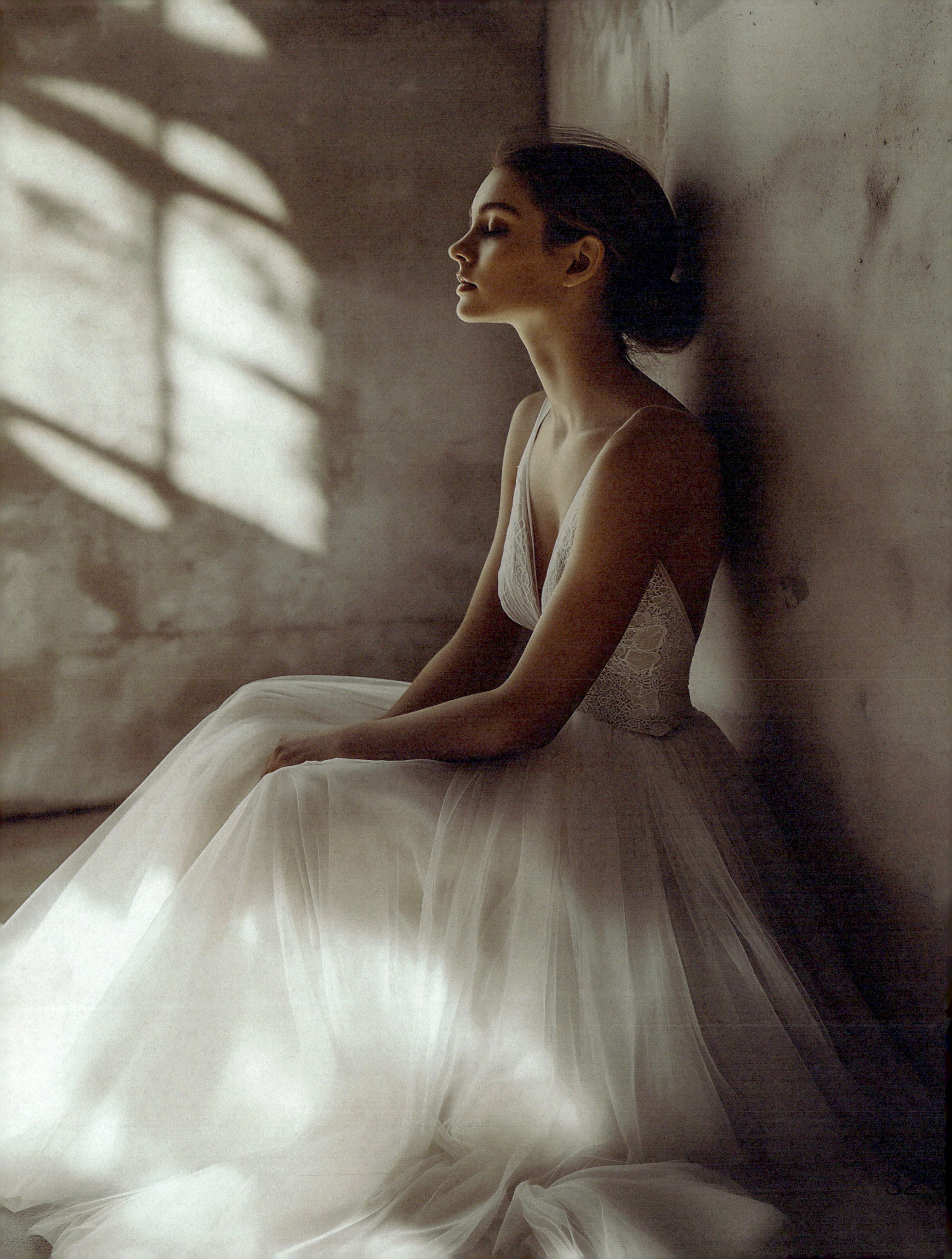

> Modern minimalist dress designs emphasize the silhouette and movement of the dress, contrasting with heavily adorned gowns. This approach allows the bride to shine without distraction.
>
> The artistry lies in the precision of the cut, the sculptural drape of the fabric, and the balance between structure and fluidity.

34

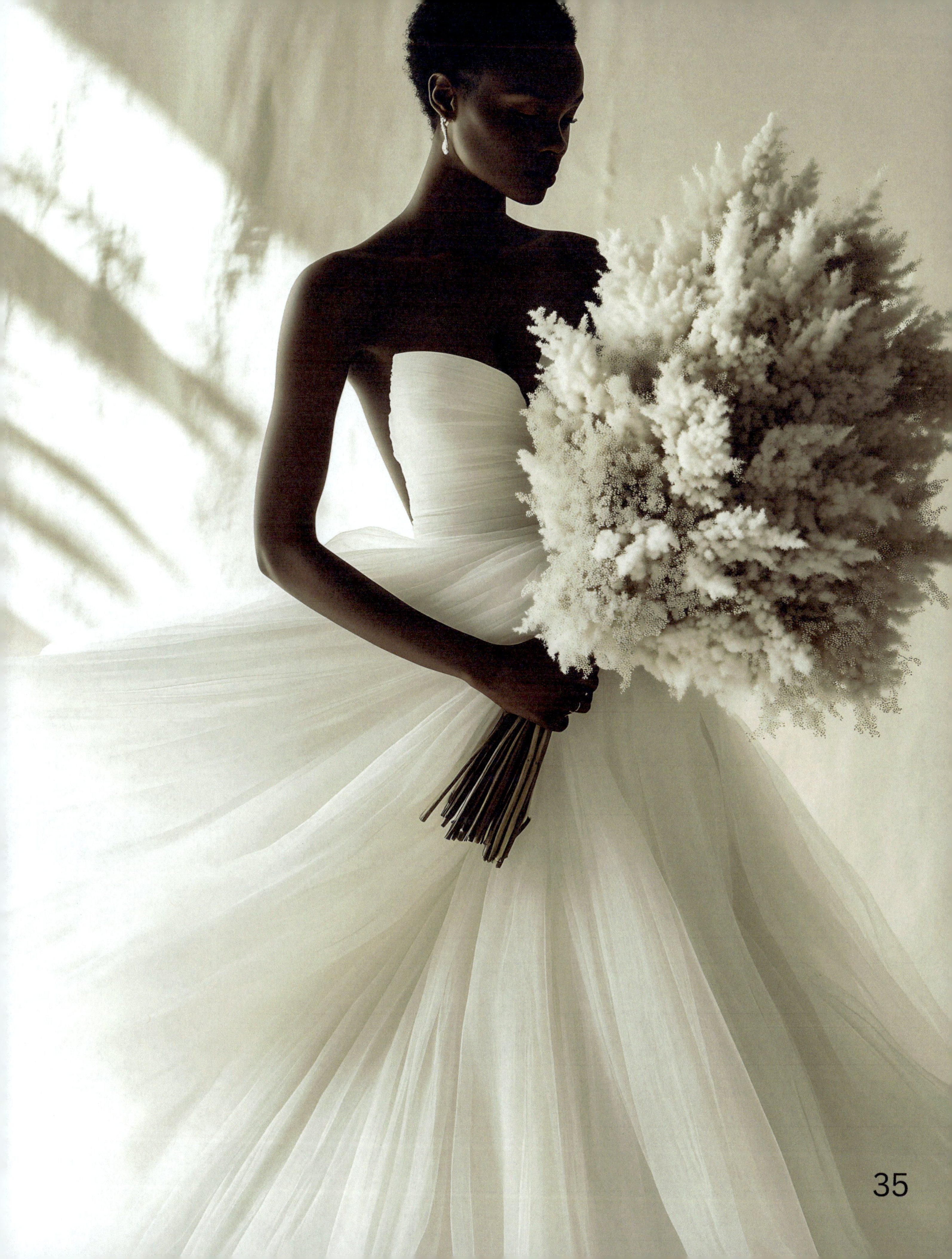

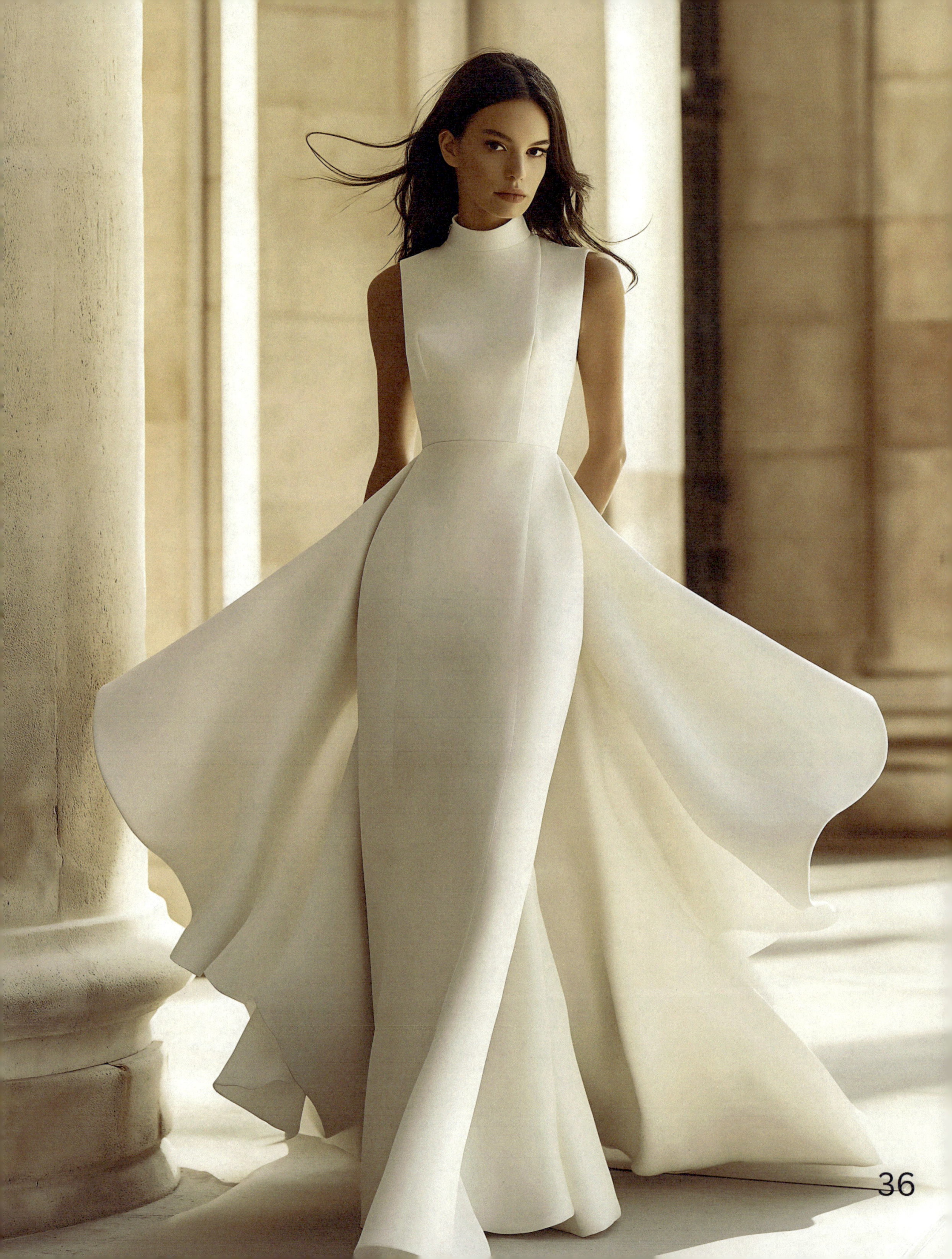

37

38

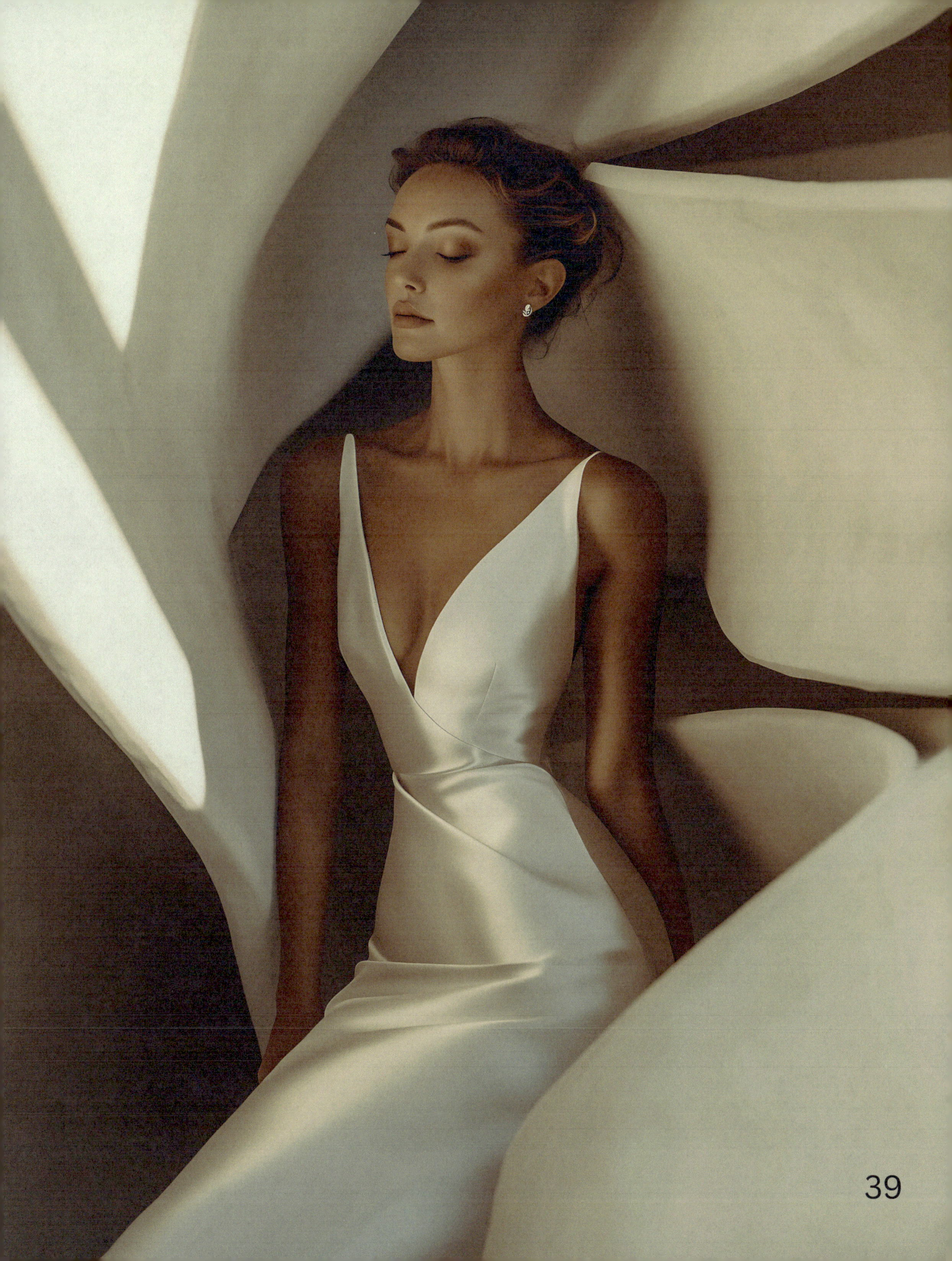

40

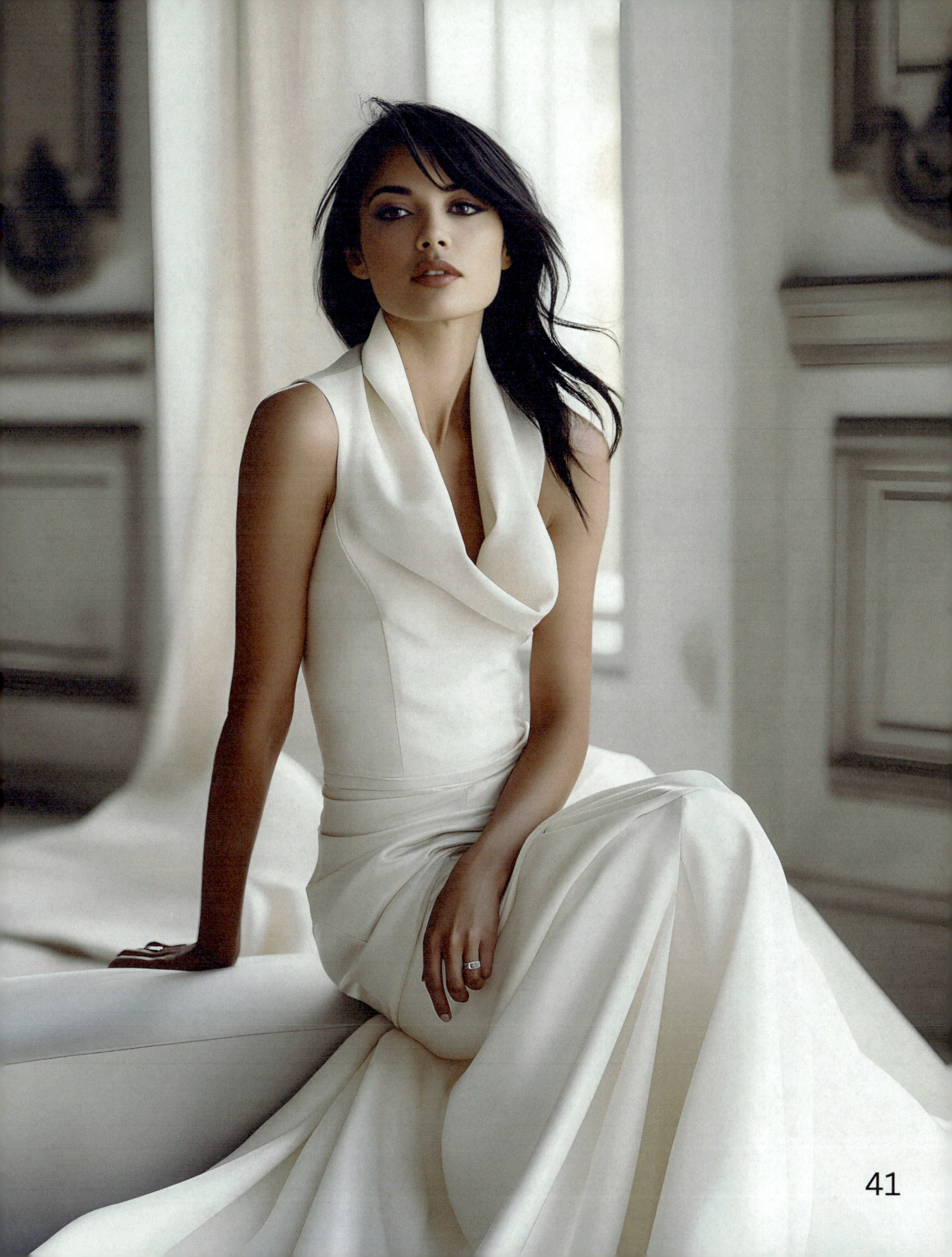

42

43

44

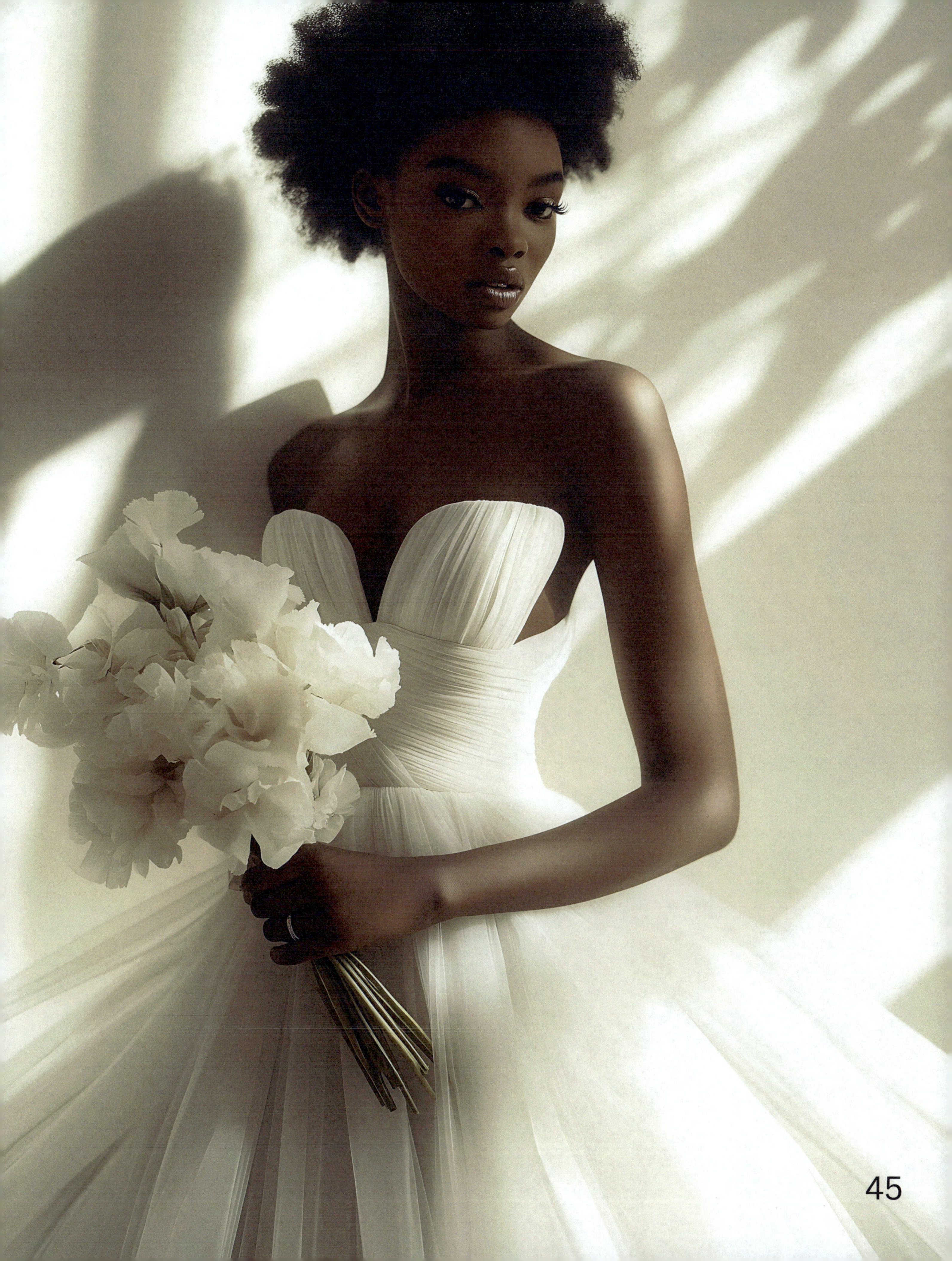

46

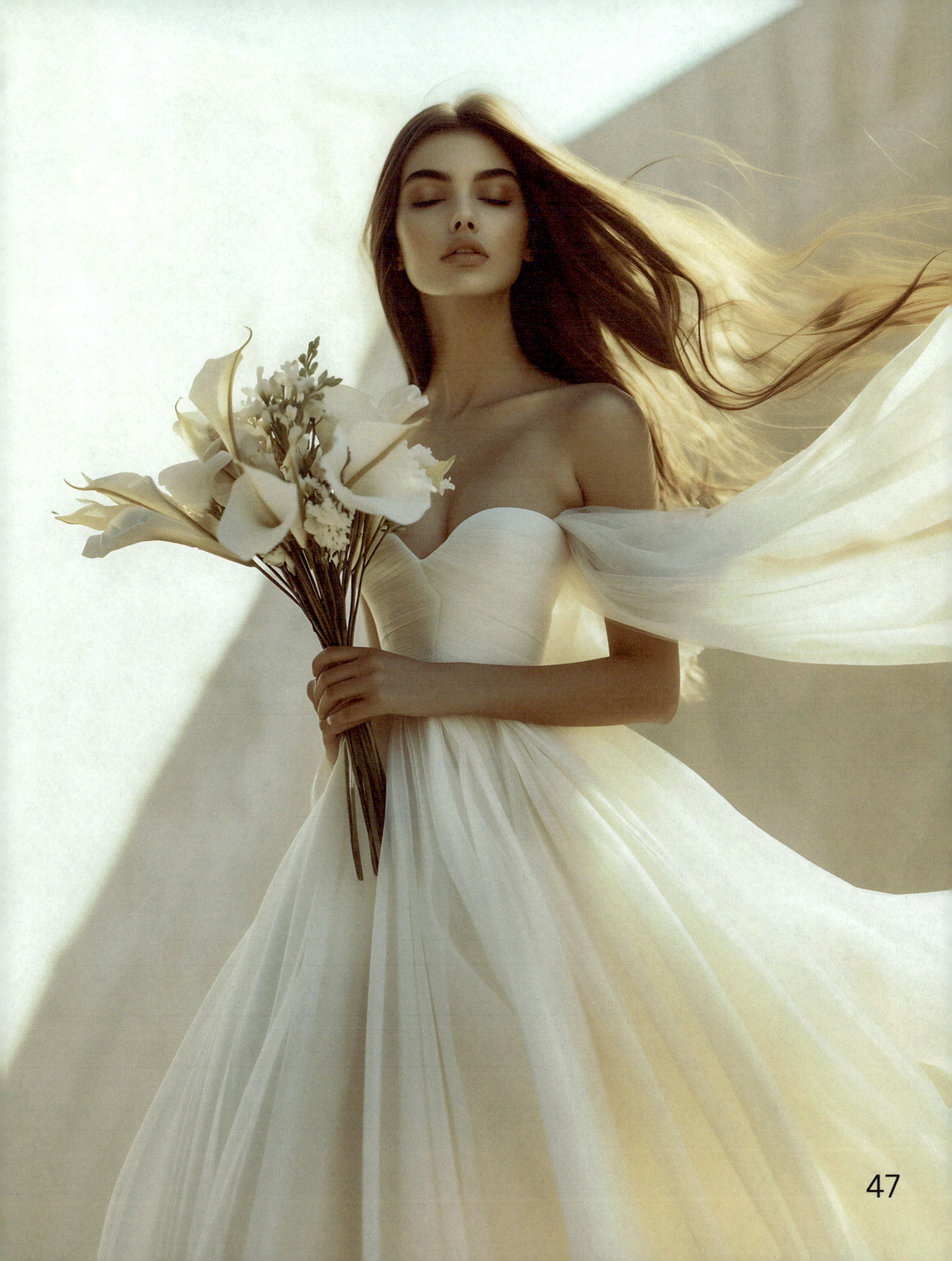

48

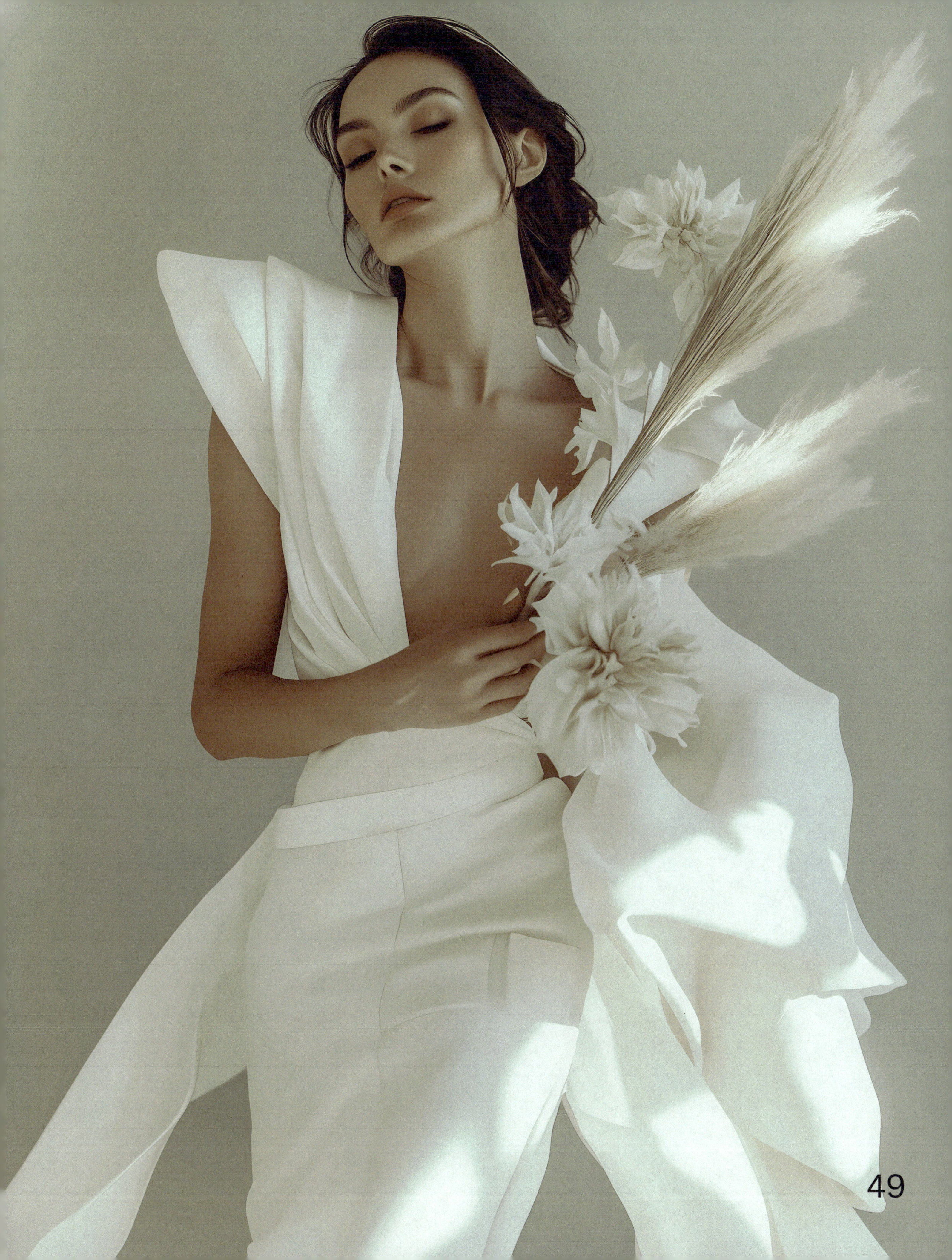

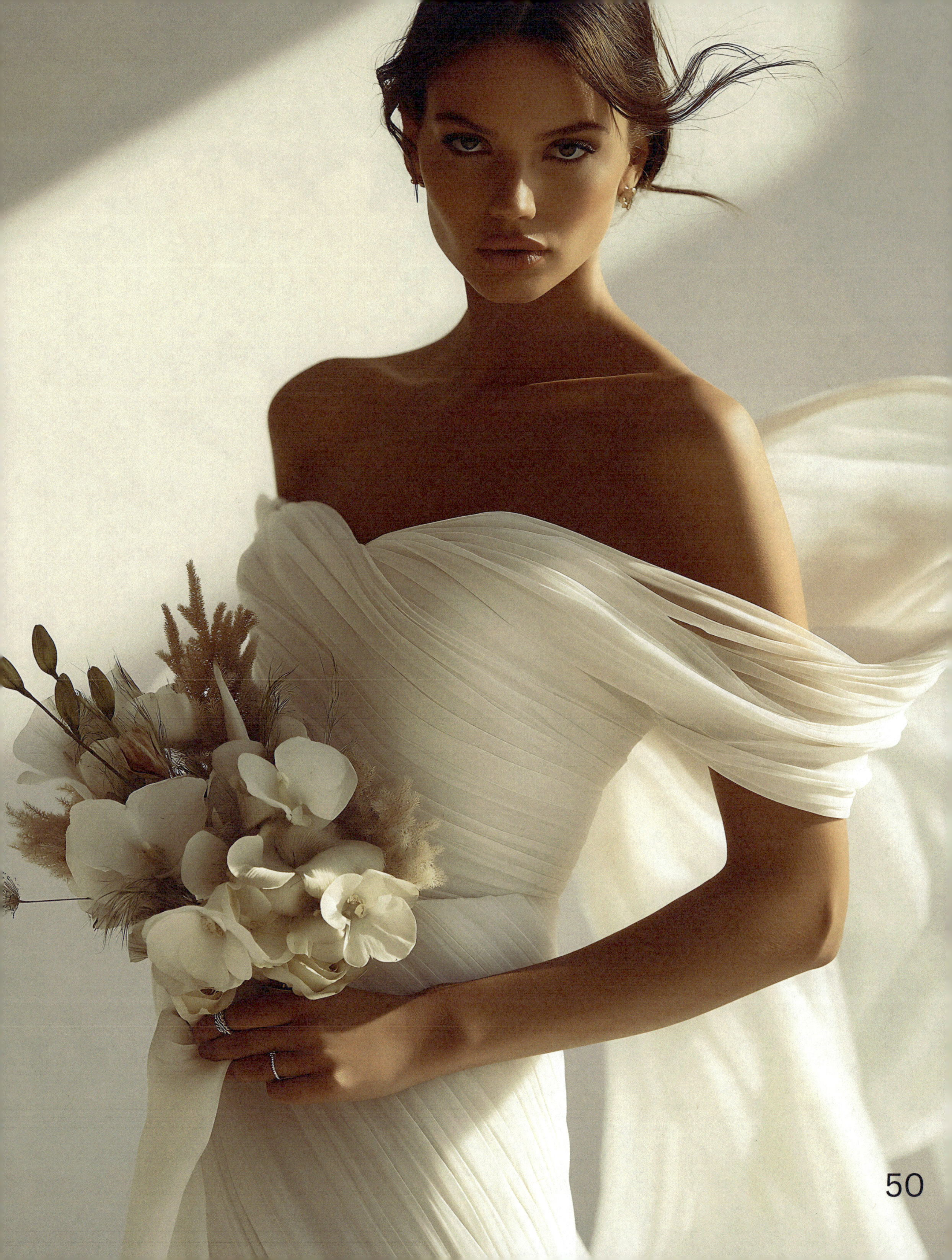

51

CHAPTER 2

MINIMALIST DRESSES WITH A UNIQUE TWIST

For the bride who dares to stand out, statement couture gowns are the ultimate expression of bold artistry and fearless fashion. Minimalism does not mean plain or predictable. Some of the most breathtaking wedding dresses embrace simplicity while incorporating one defining element that makes them unforgettable. Whether it's an unexpected backless design, an oversized bow, an asymmetrical drape, or a dramatic cape, these gowns capture attention while maintaining a refined aesthetic.

This chapter explores the art of understated drama, the delicate balance between minimalism and statement design. It showcases dresses that play with proportions, movement, and structure, proving that even simple gowns can have an element of surprise.

5.

> *These gowns make the most impactful statement with confidence, simplicity, and exceptional craftsmanship.*

55

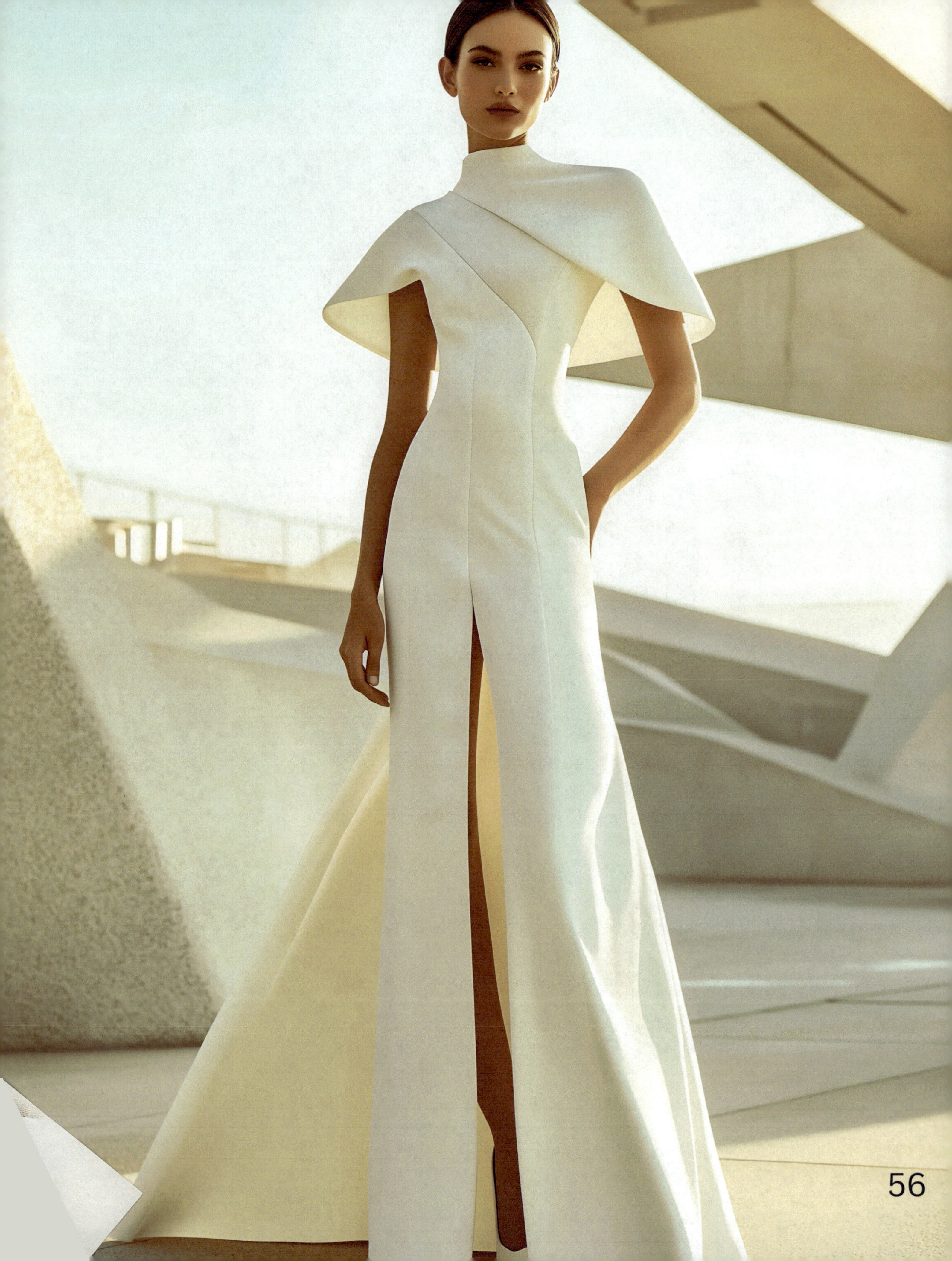

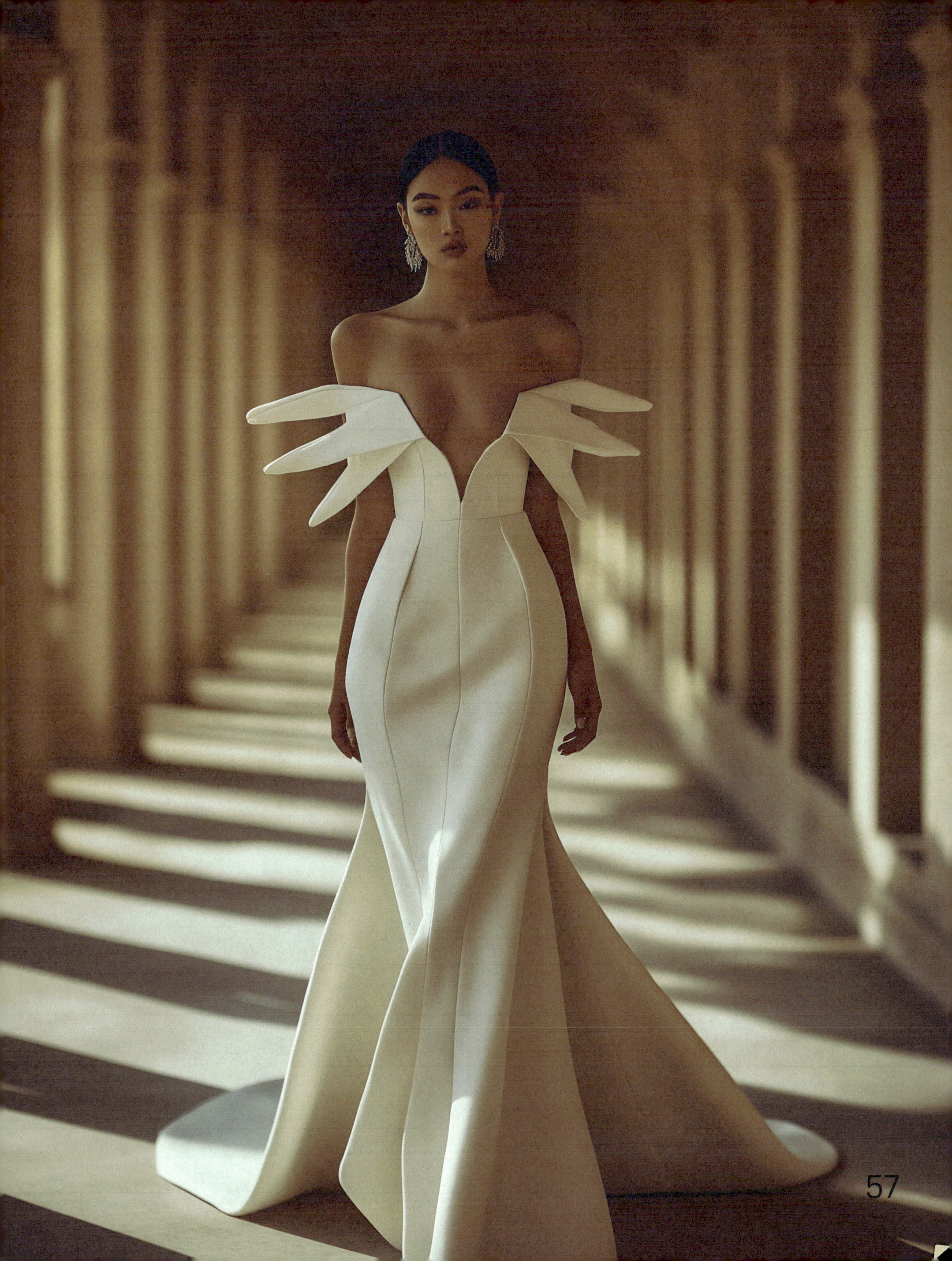

58

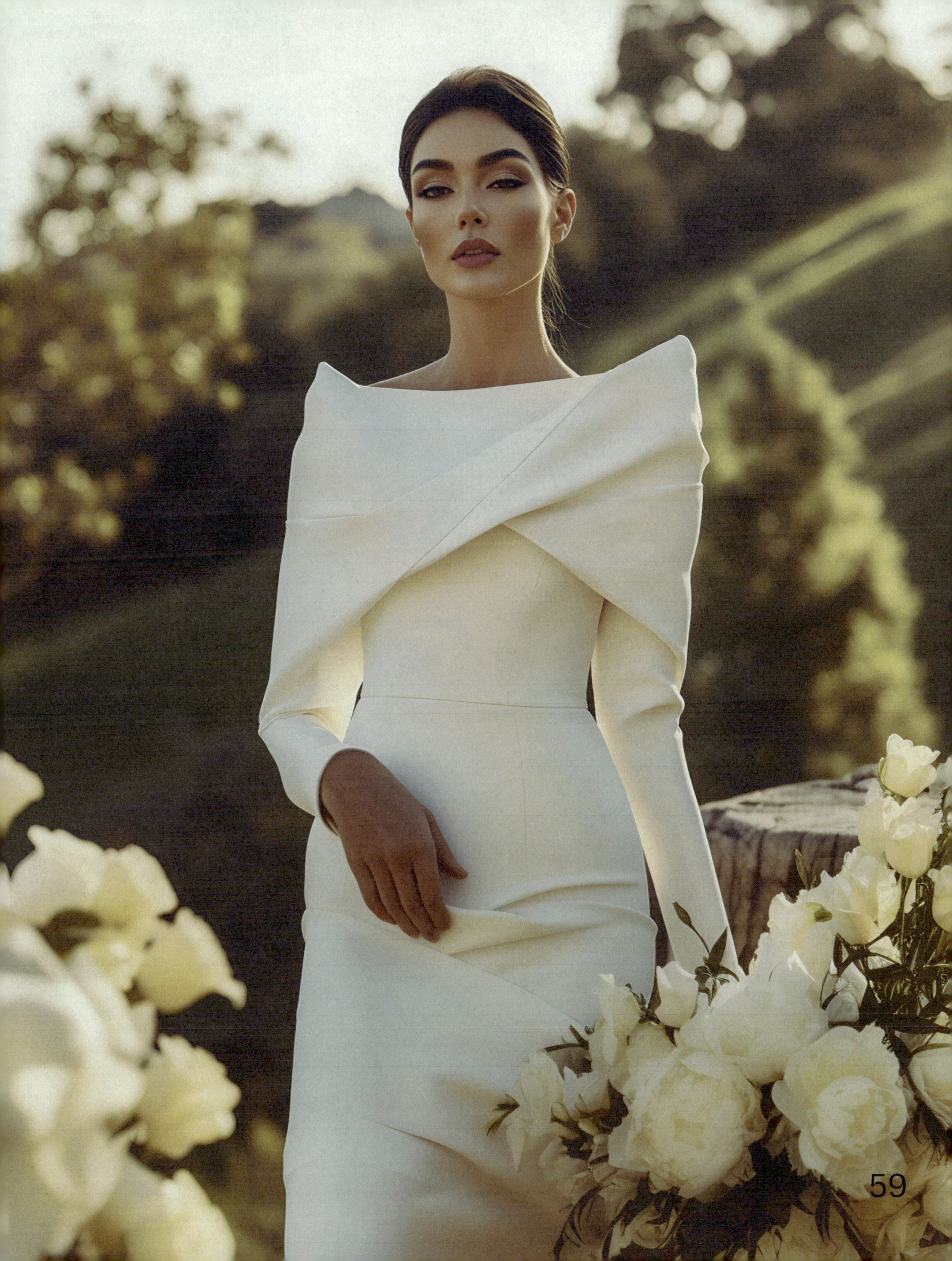

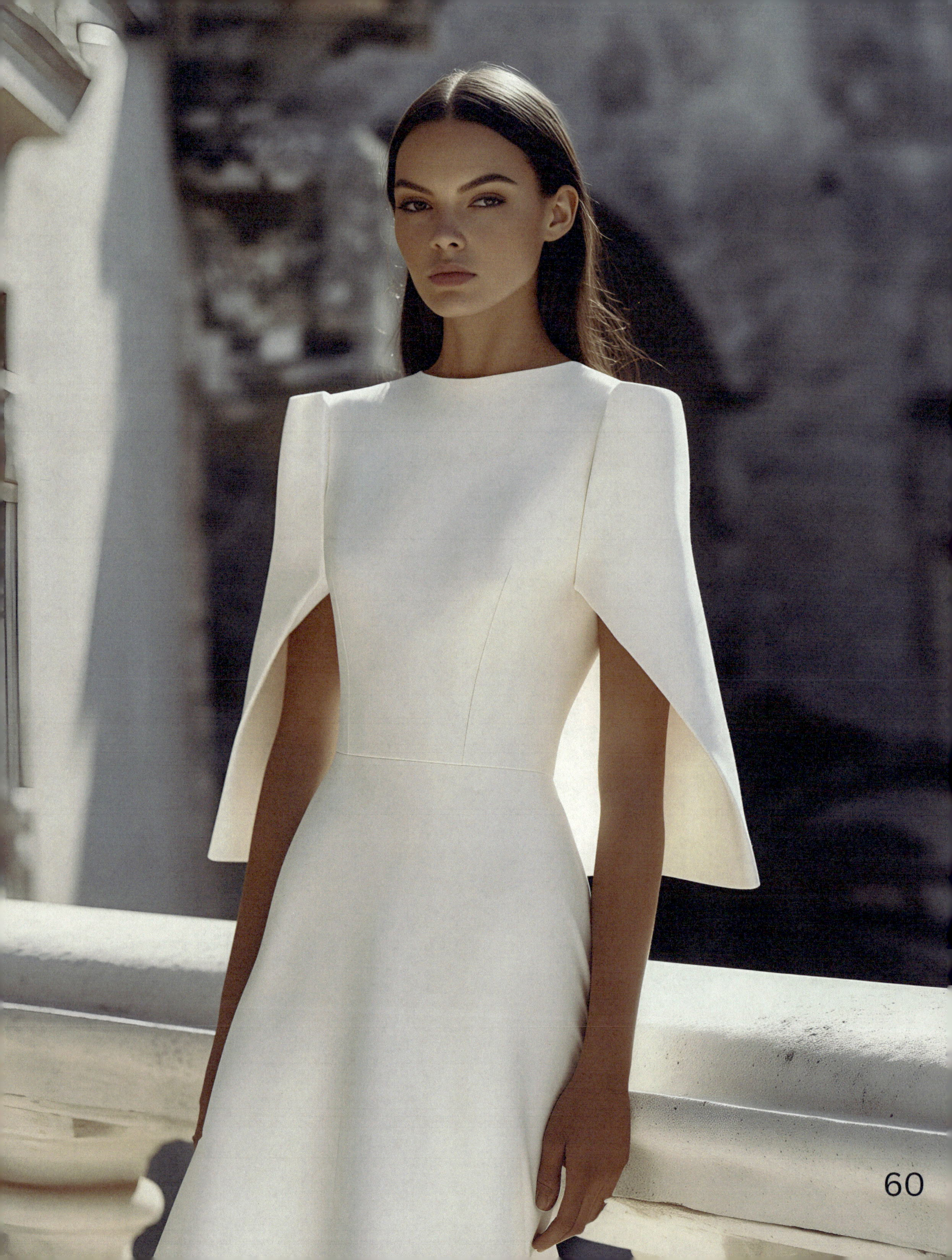

> Unlike traditional bridal styles, statement gowns push the boundaries of design.
>
> They feature voluminous ballgown skirts, dramatic ruffles, oversized bows, intricate 3D embellishments, and sculptural elements that turn fabric into art. Designers often experiment with asymmetry, exaggerated proportions, and high-fashion drama, ensuring each dress is worn and experienced.

STATEMENT COUTURE GOWNS

"

These designs draw inspiration from theatrical runway shows, haute couture collections, and historical influences reinterpreted through a modern lens. Each piece is crafted to captivate.

A statement couture gown is for the bride who embraces fashion as a form of self-expression, a woman who isn't afraid to be the center of attention, to embrace the unconventional, and to celebrate her wedding day in a way that is uniquely her own. These gowns remind us that fashion is not just about clothing but emotion, storytelling, and unforgettable moments.

"

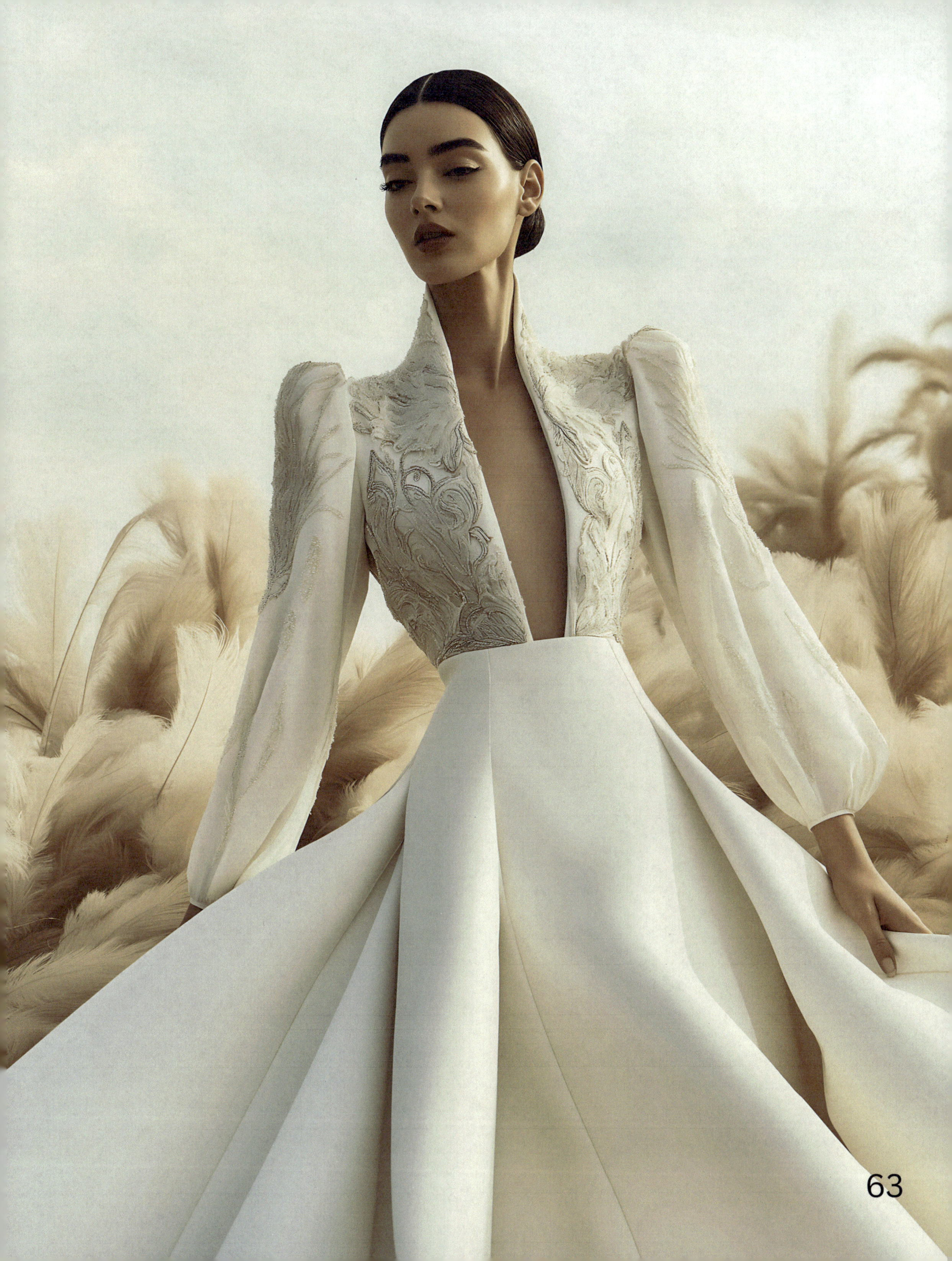

64

The Power of Statement Couture

—❝—

A wedding gown is more than just a dress, it is a work of art, a reflection of personality, and a bold declaration of style. Statement couture gowns take this philosophy to the extreme, embracing theatrical proportions, avant-garde design, and breathtaking detail to create a moment of pure fashion drama.

—❞—

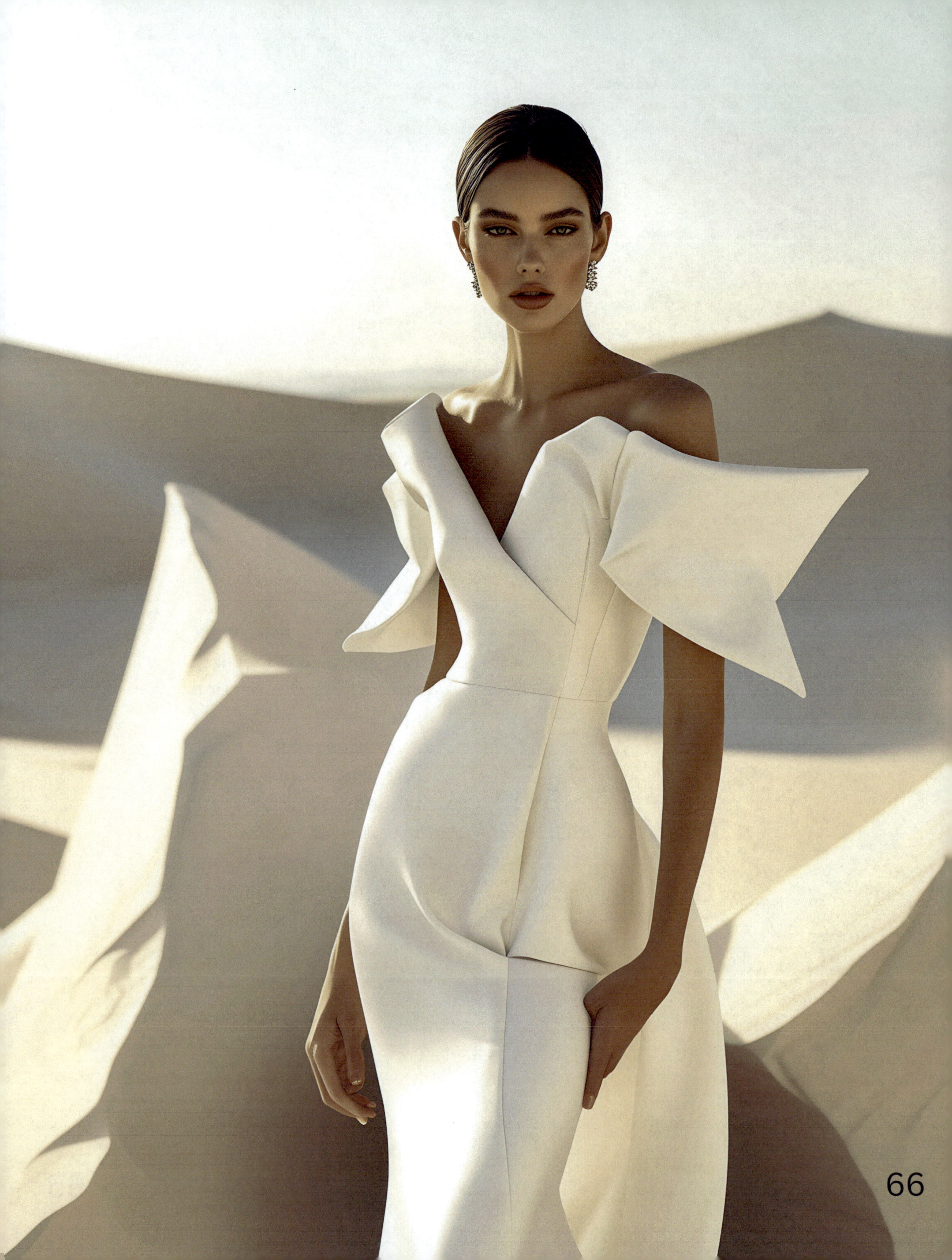

67

— 66 ———

Statement gowns allow brides to depart from tradition and embrace the extraordinary, whether inspired by baroque opulence, avant-garde fashion, or runway couture.

Couture gowns are designed to captivate. From gravity-defying silhouettes, extravagant sleeves, and delicate yet voluminous fabric create movement and dimension. Every element is intentional, from metallic-thread embroidery to daring asymmetry and sculptural draping, transforming the bride into a living masterpiece.

For those who aspire to make an unforgettable entrance, these designs demonstrate that drama is always in style.

——————— 99 —

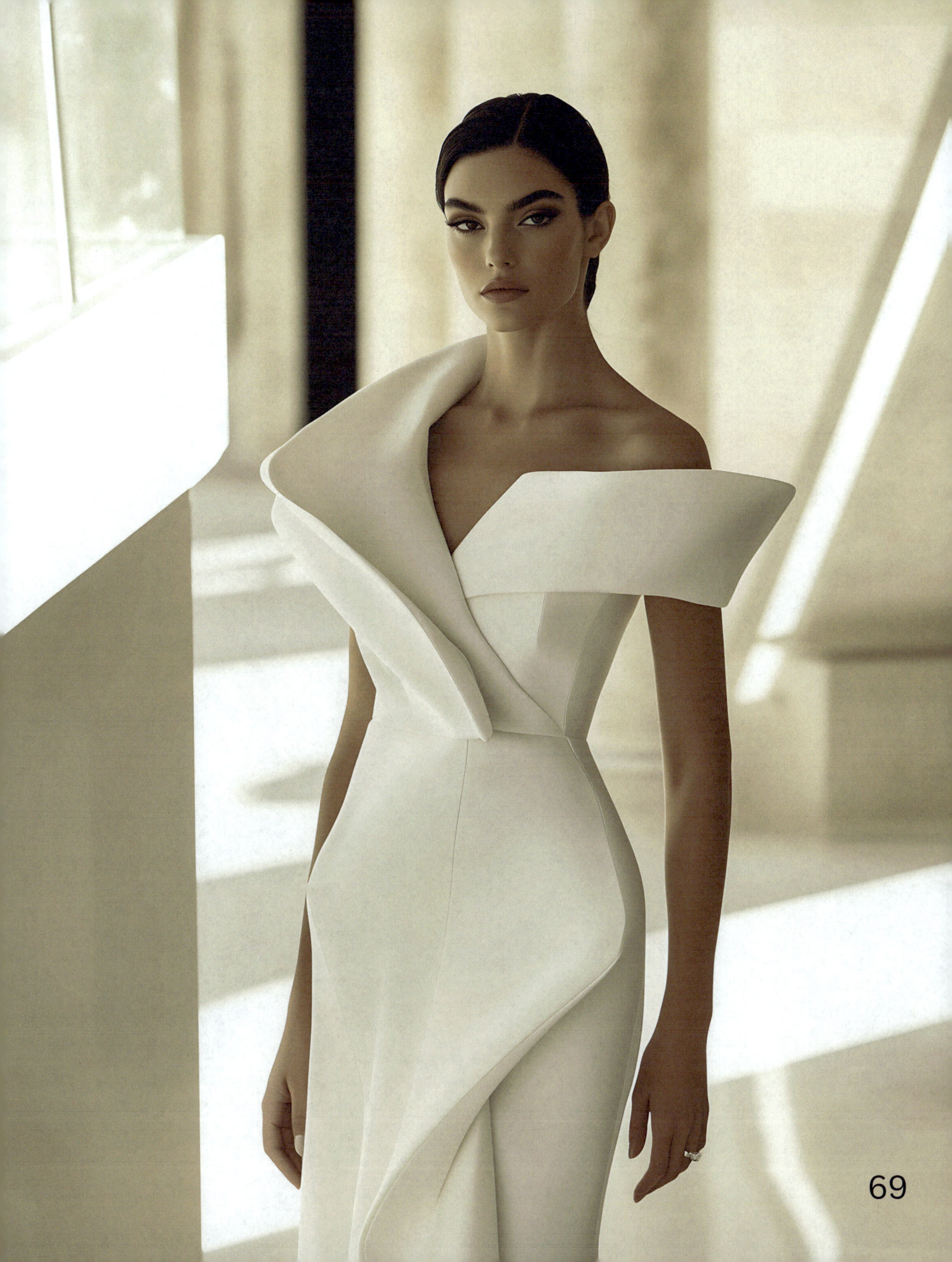

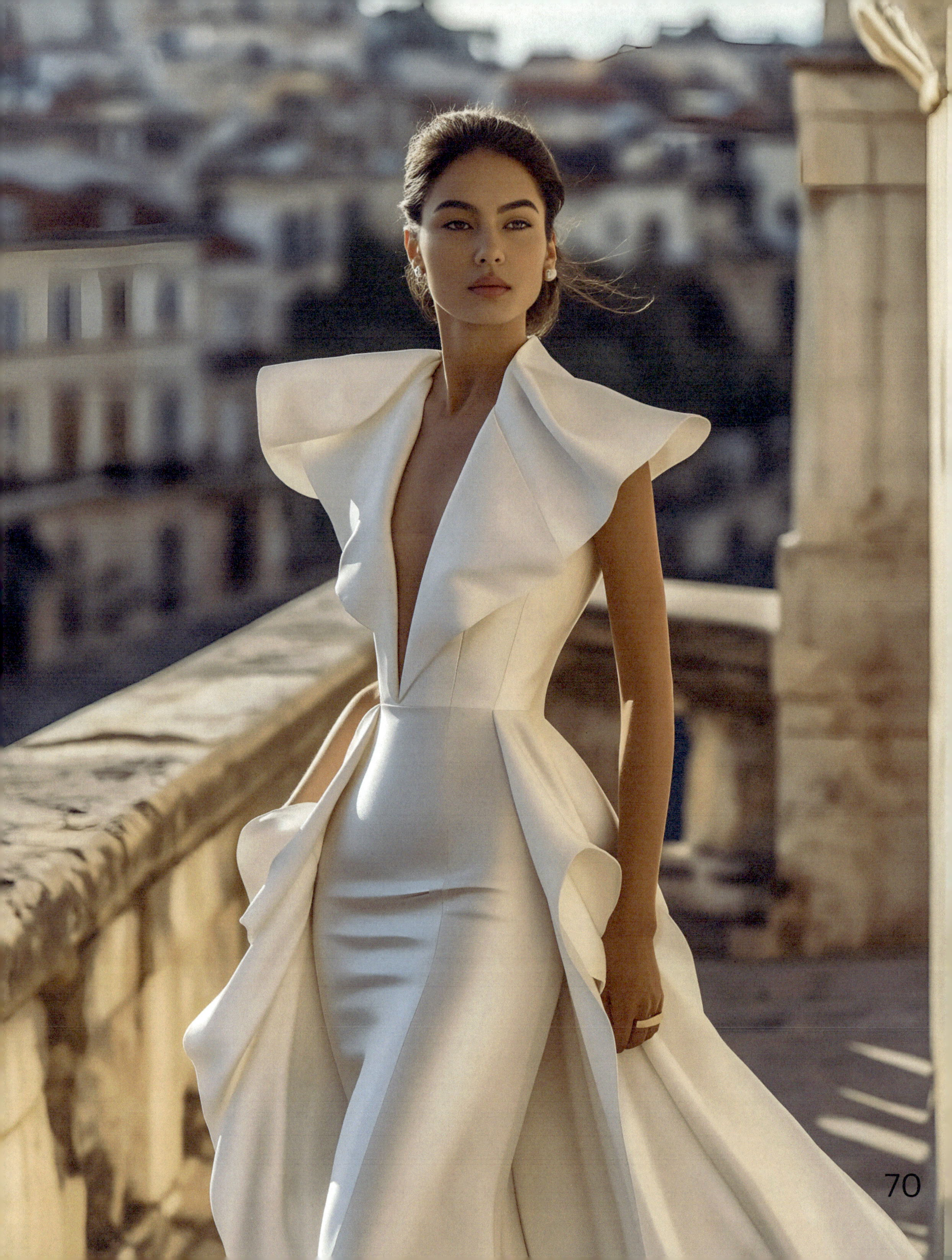

> Fashion icons and couture designers have long recognized the power of drama in bridal wear, each piece an exploration of grandeur and artistry. These gowns are not just worn, they are experienced.

CHAPTER 3

SIMPLE COUTURE

— 66 ———

In a world where bridal fashion is often synonymous with exaggerated volume, intricate beading, and complex lacework, there is something truly breathtaking about the beauty of simple couture wedding gowns. These dresses focus on understated elegance, embracing the philosophy that less is more. They may forgo heavy embellishments, but the craftsmanship, fabric choice, and fit elevate them to the highest levels of fashion.

A simple couture gown showcases flawless tailoring, luxurious fabric, and clean lines. These gowns highlight the bride's natural beauty and poise rather than distract from it. The simplicity lies in the dress's silhouette, the quality of the fabric, and the way it flows gracefully without needing much embellishment to make a statement. These gowns celebrate refined beauty and cater to brides who appreciate timelessness over trends.

——— 99 —

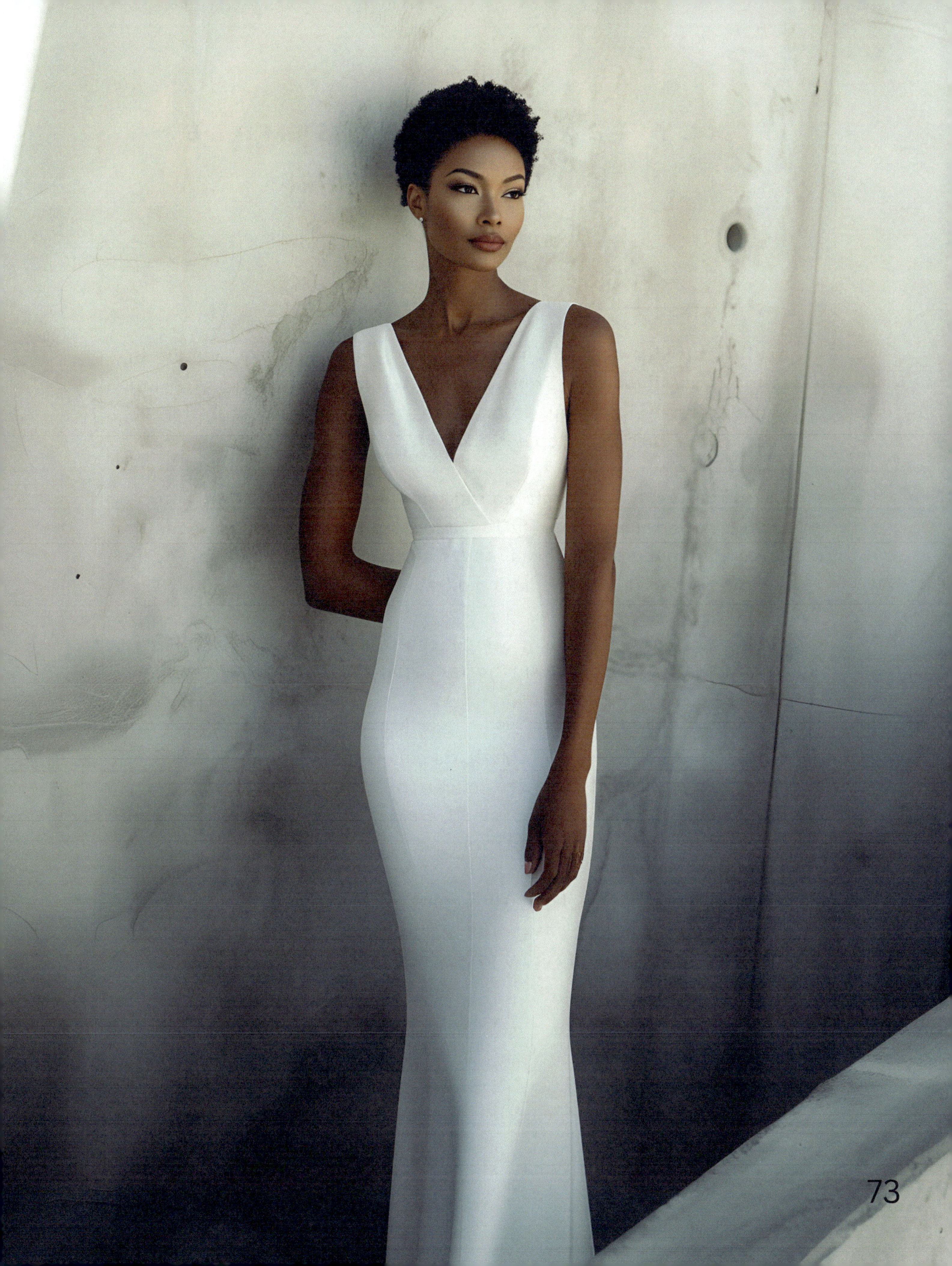

KEY FEATURES OF SIMPLE COUTURE GOWNS

— 66 ———————

Sculptural Silhouettes: *The beauty of simple couture lies in its minimalist silhouette. From classic A-line to sheath styles and column dresses, the focus is on clean, smooth lines that flatter the body without over-the-top details.*

Luxurious Fabrics: *Simple couture wedding dresses often feature rich fabrics such as silk satin, crepe, or mikado, which lend the dress an understated sheen and fluidity. The material is key to creating a dress that feels both modern and timeless.*

Flawless Fit and Tailoring: *Simple couture gowns are meticulously tailored to perfection, ensuring they hug the body in all the right places.*

Subtle, Unique Details: *Minimalistic gowns feature tasteful touches, such as a sleek keyhole back, delicate silk buttons, or a small lace trim along the hem. These small elements add interest without detracting from the gown's elegance.*

Timeless Beauty: *Simple couture gowns never go out of style. Their classic, refined nature ensures they will always remain relevant, no matter how the bridal fashion industry evolves.*

——————— 99 —

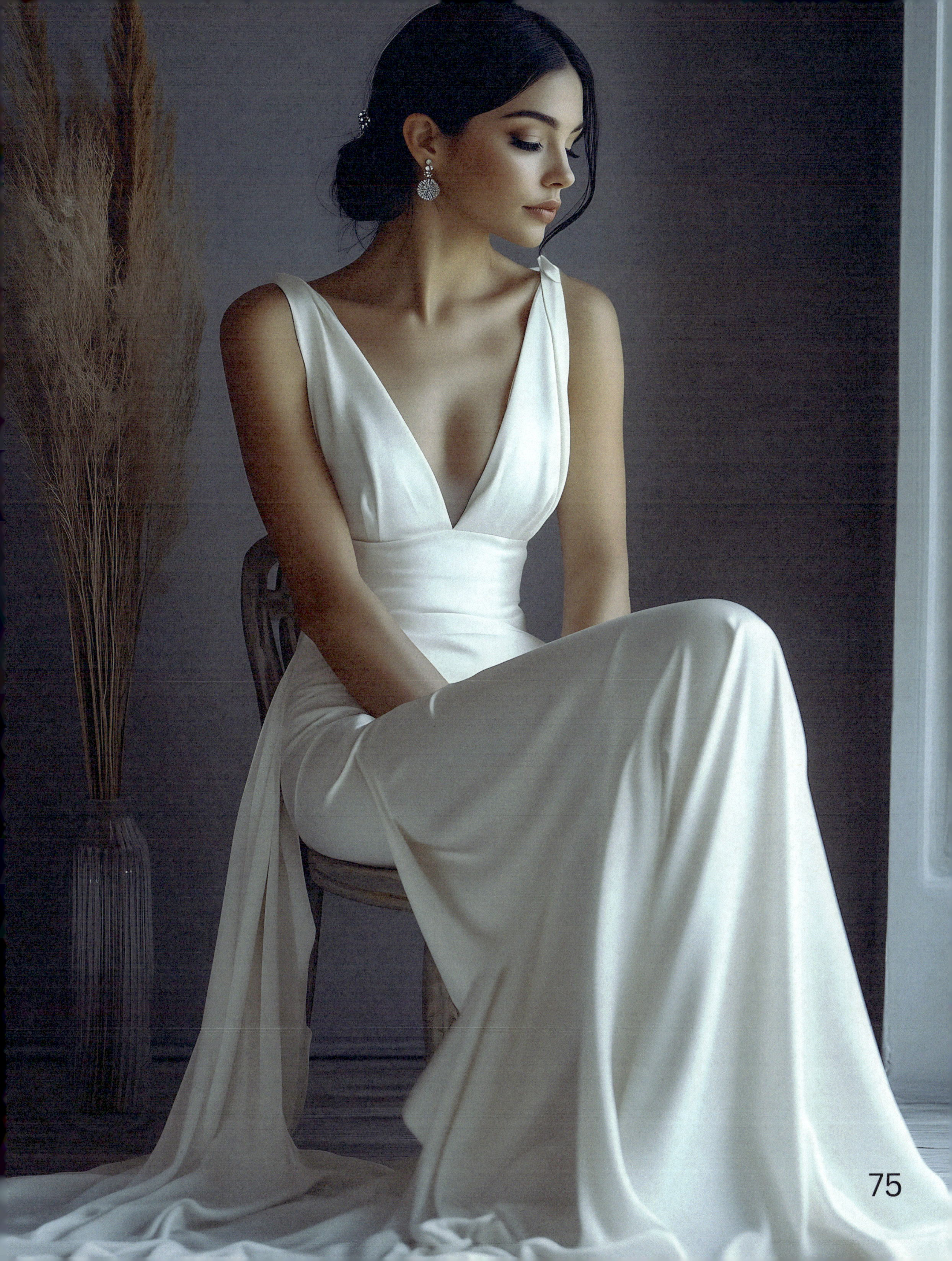

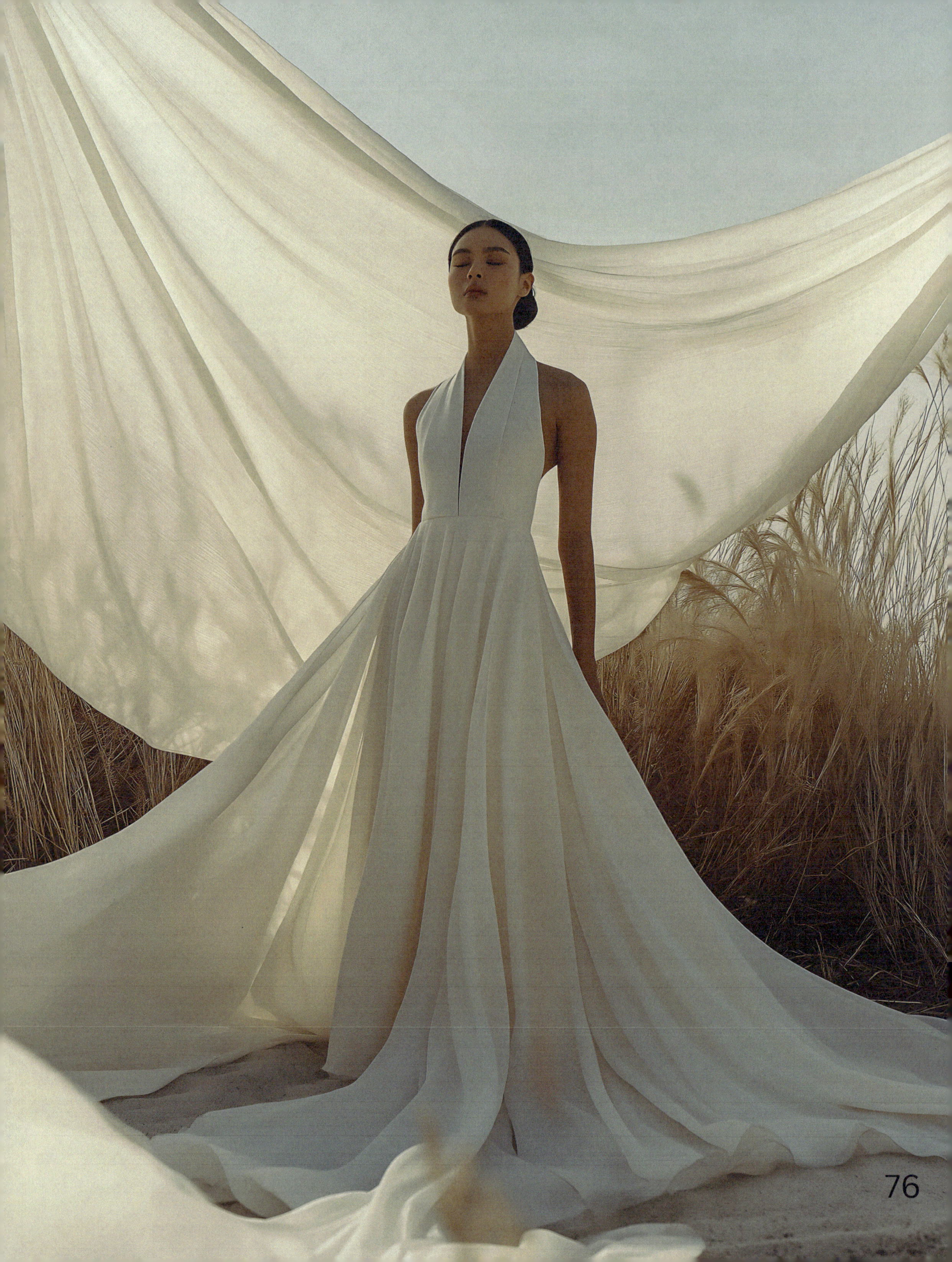

77

78

79

> Simple couture wedding gowns are perfect for brides who value timeless elegance, comfort, and sophistication. They provide a polished, refined look while allowing the bride to feel completely at ease.

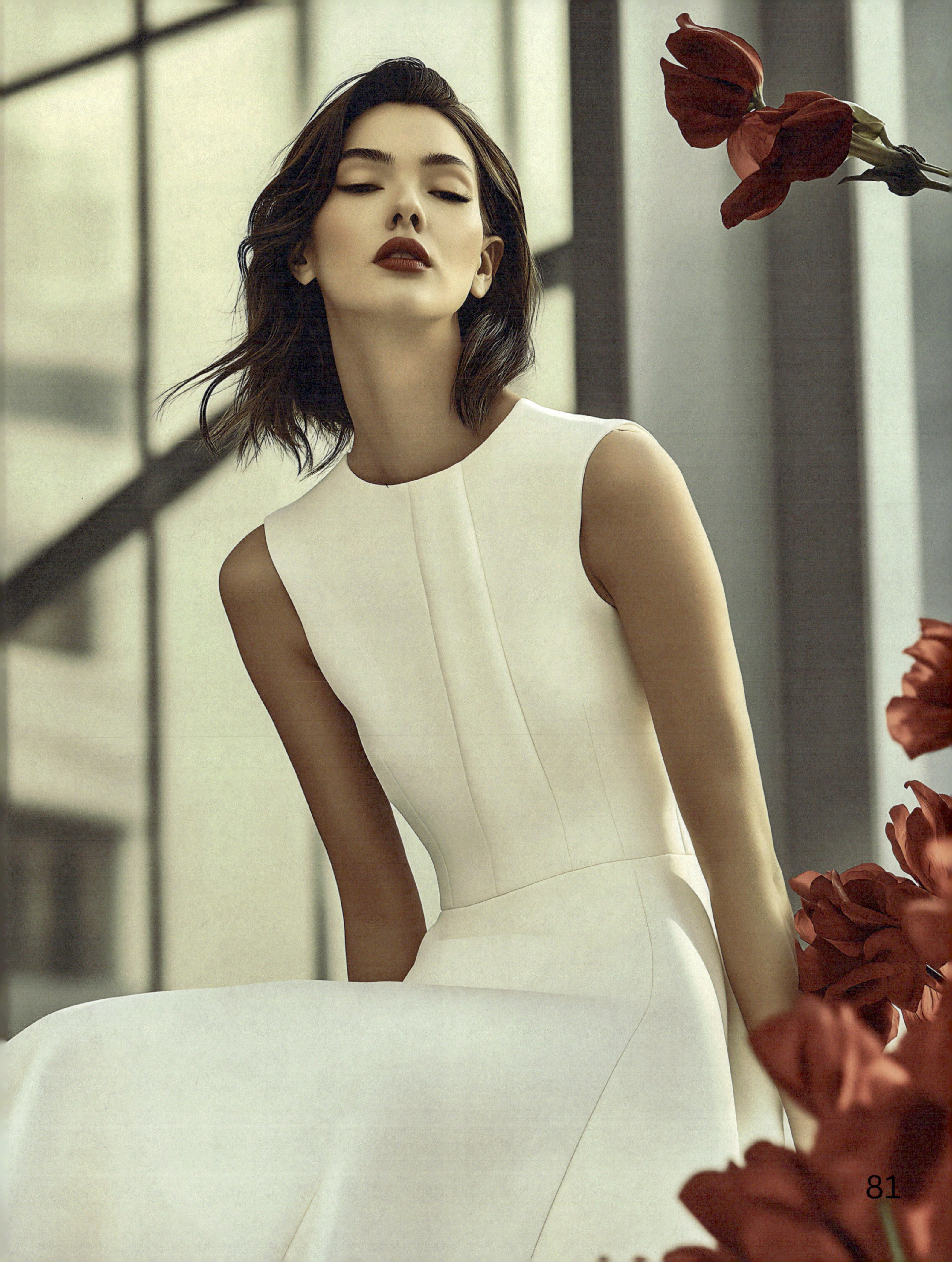

82

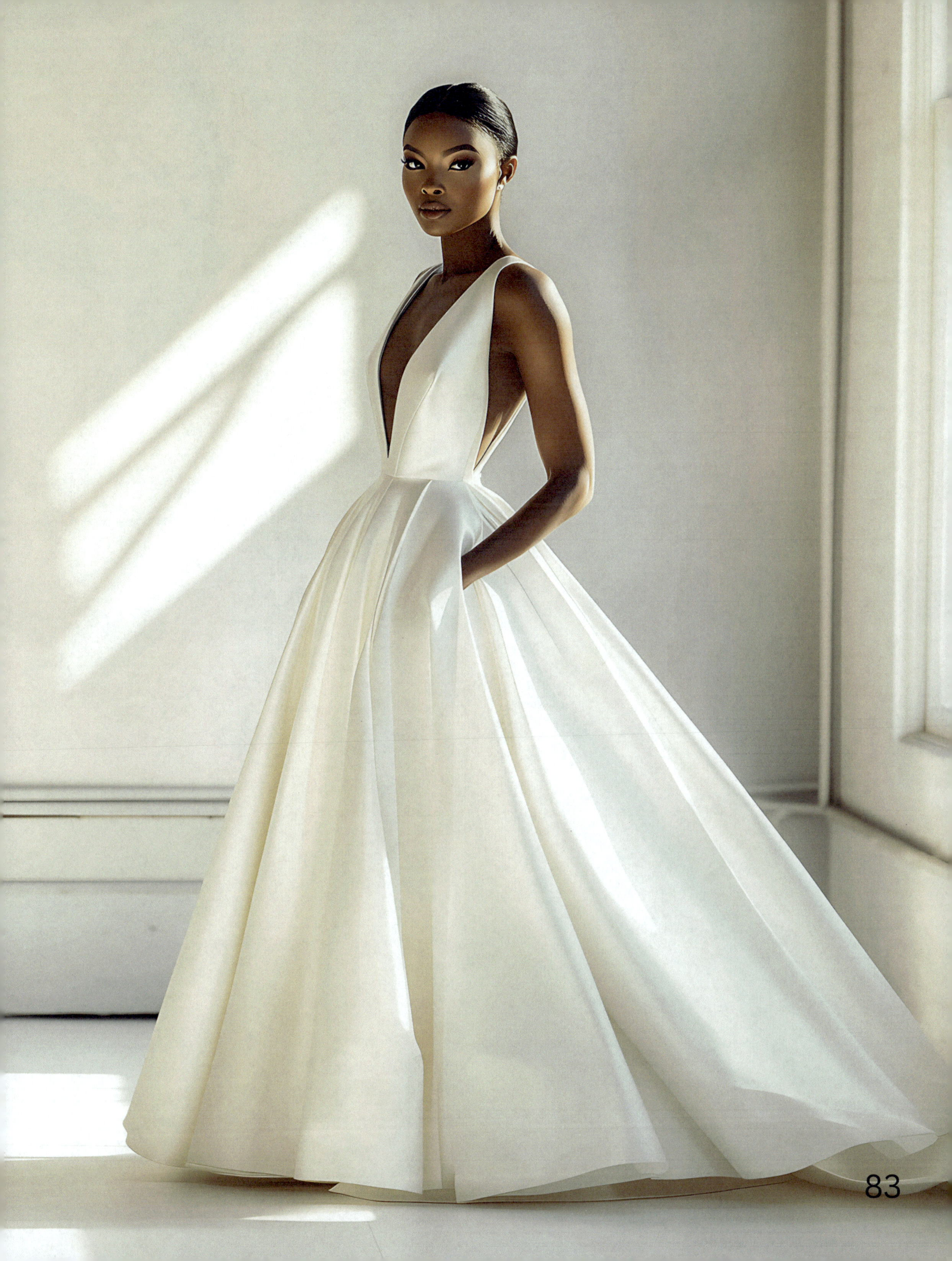

84

85

86

87

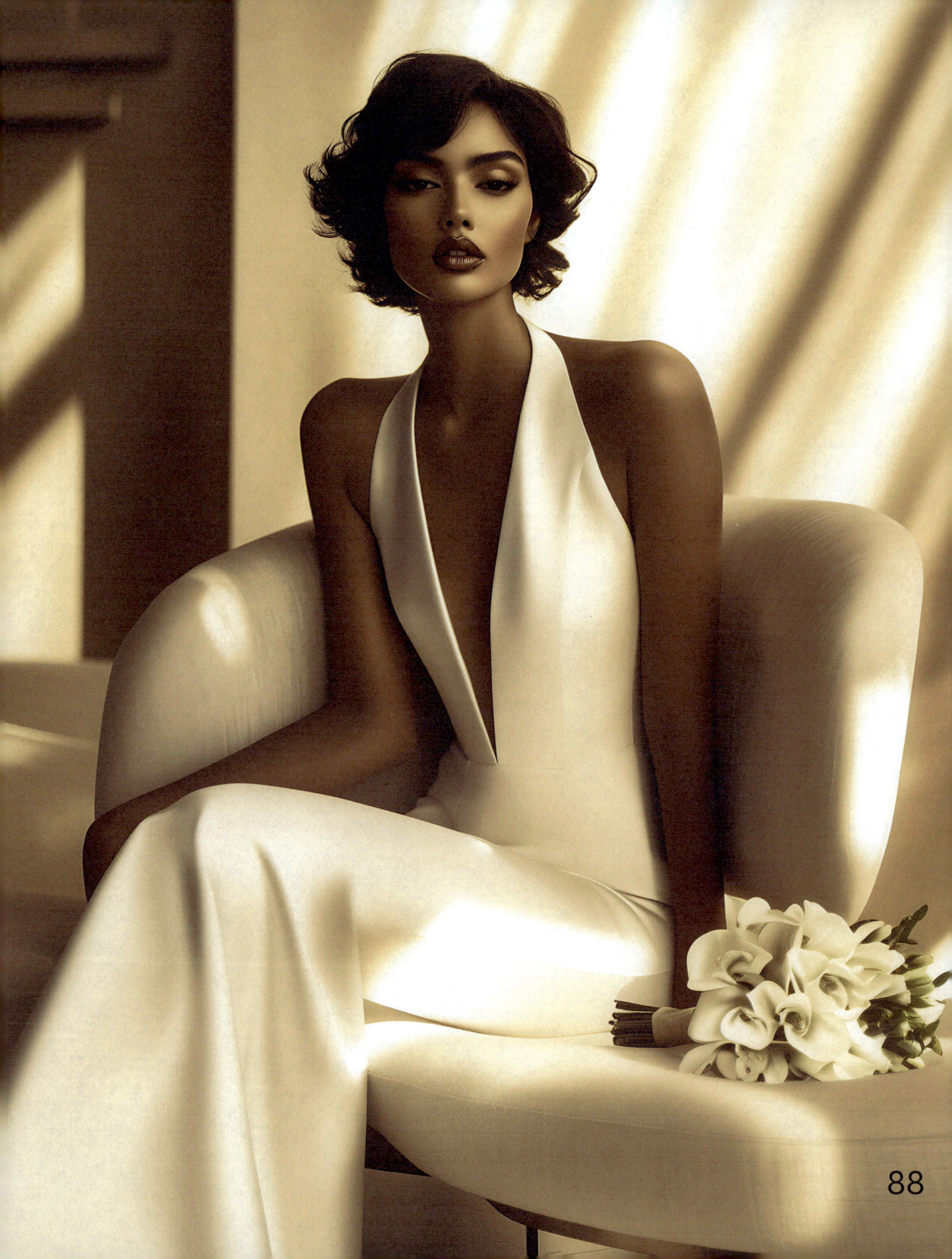

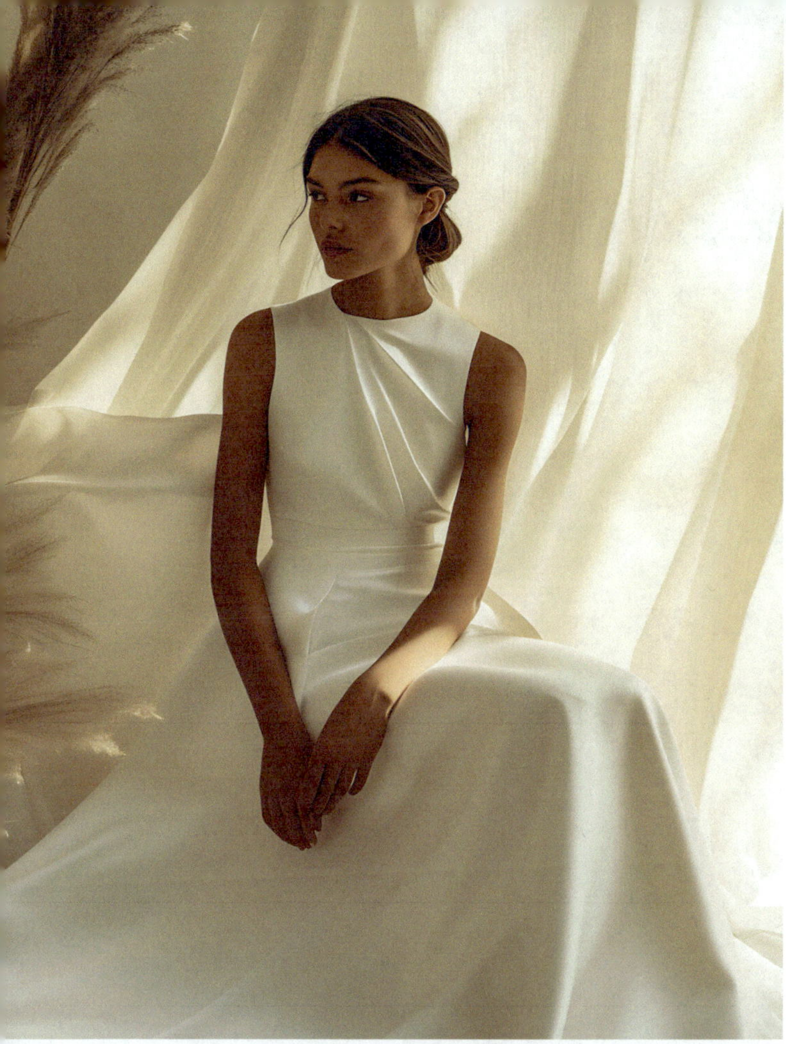

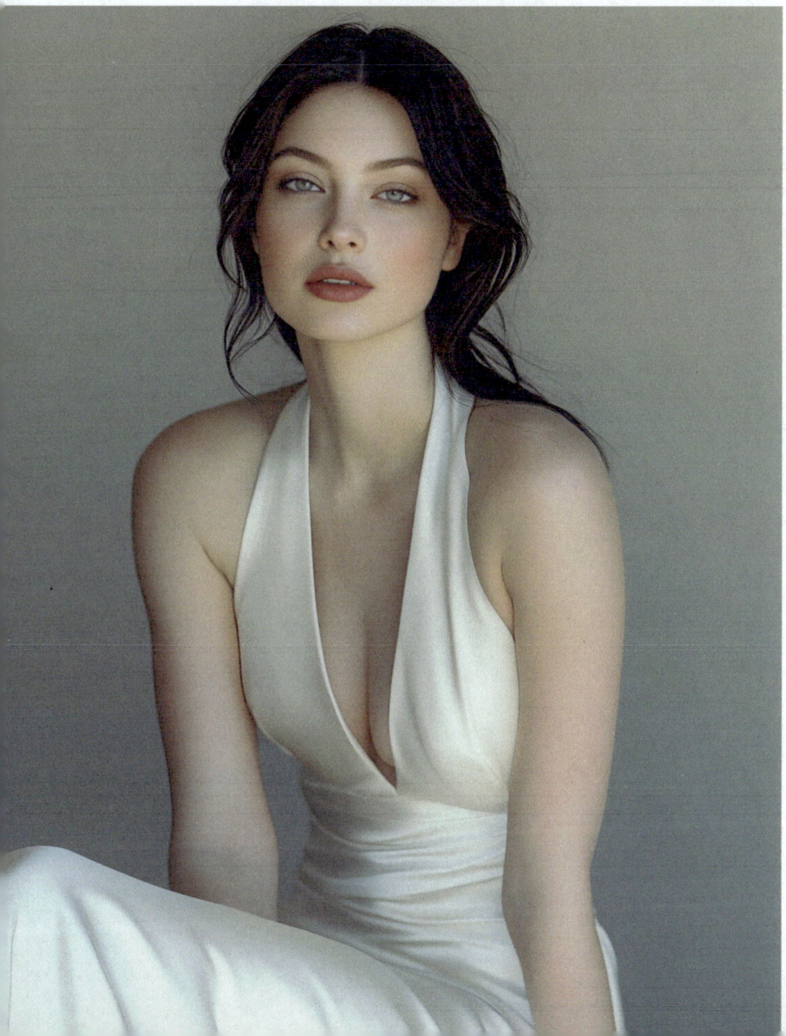

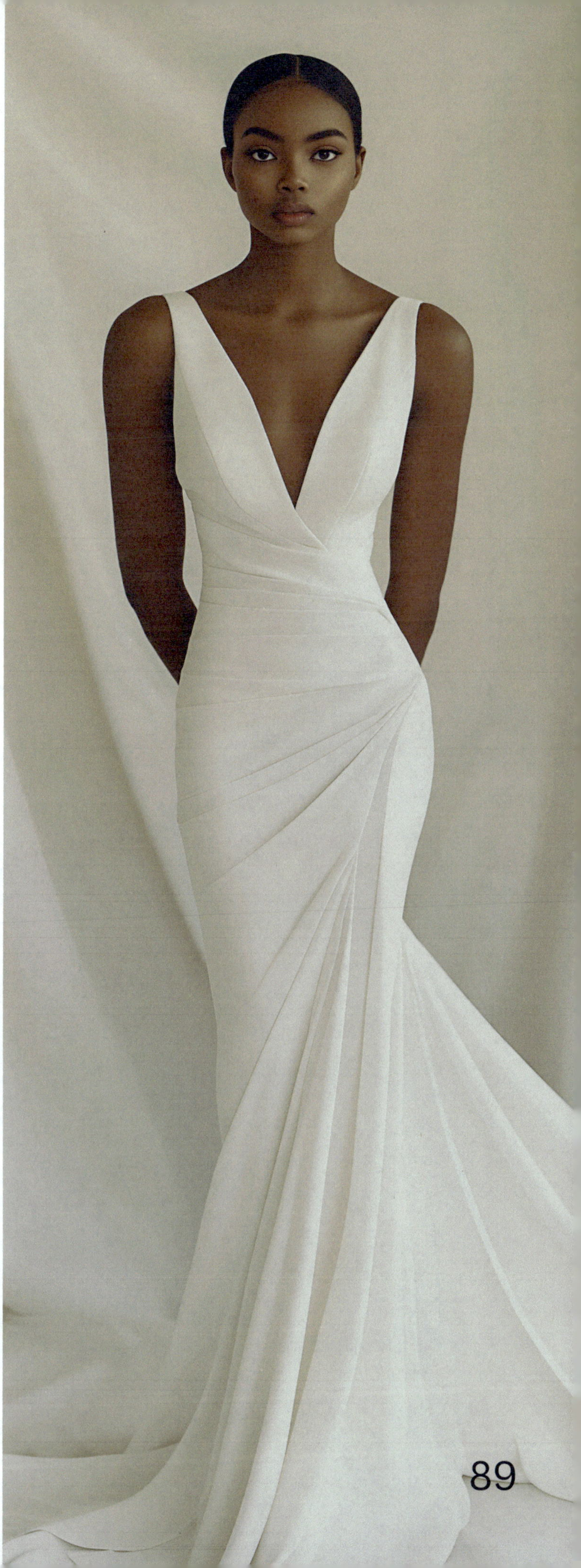

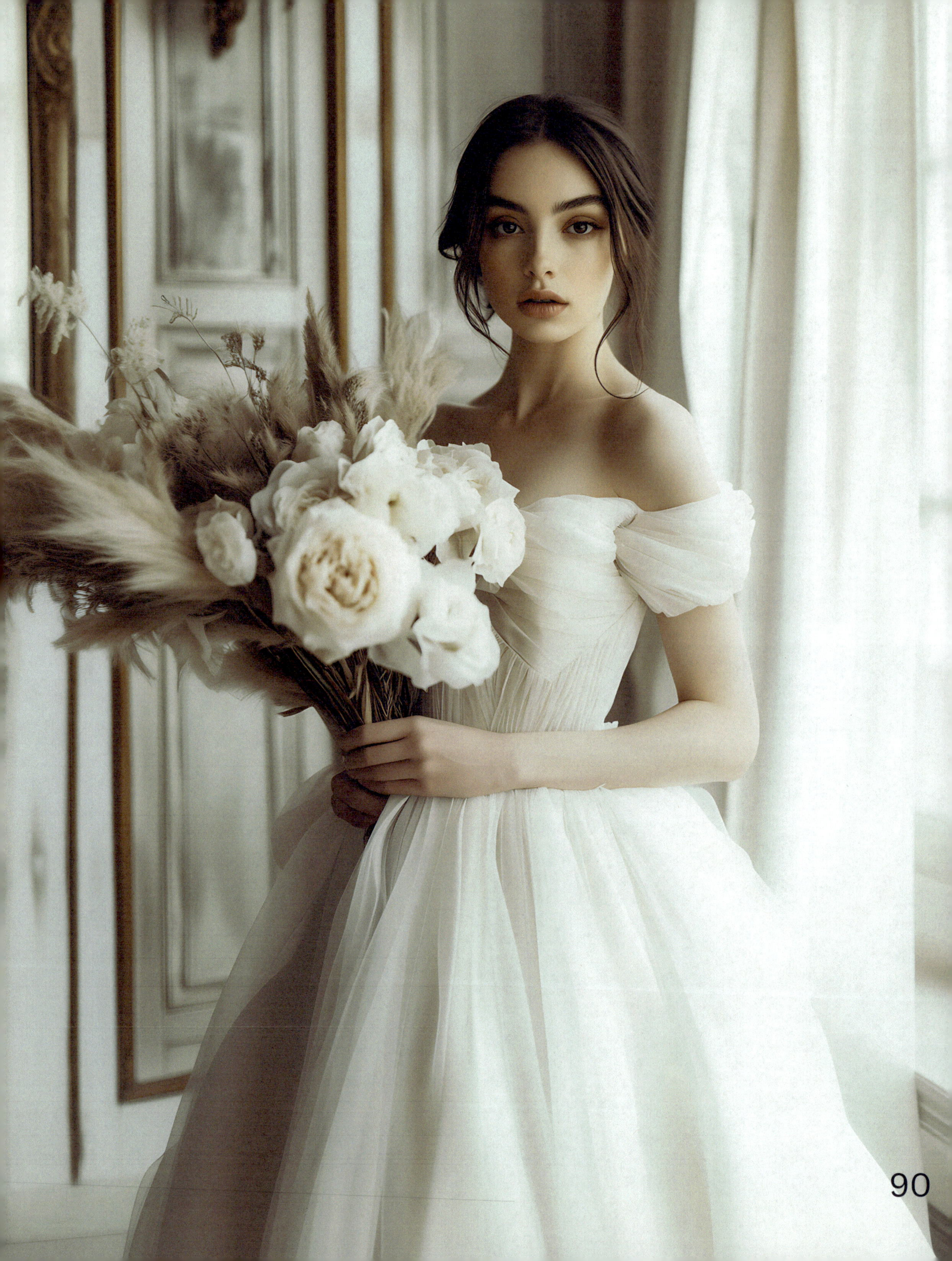

91

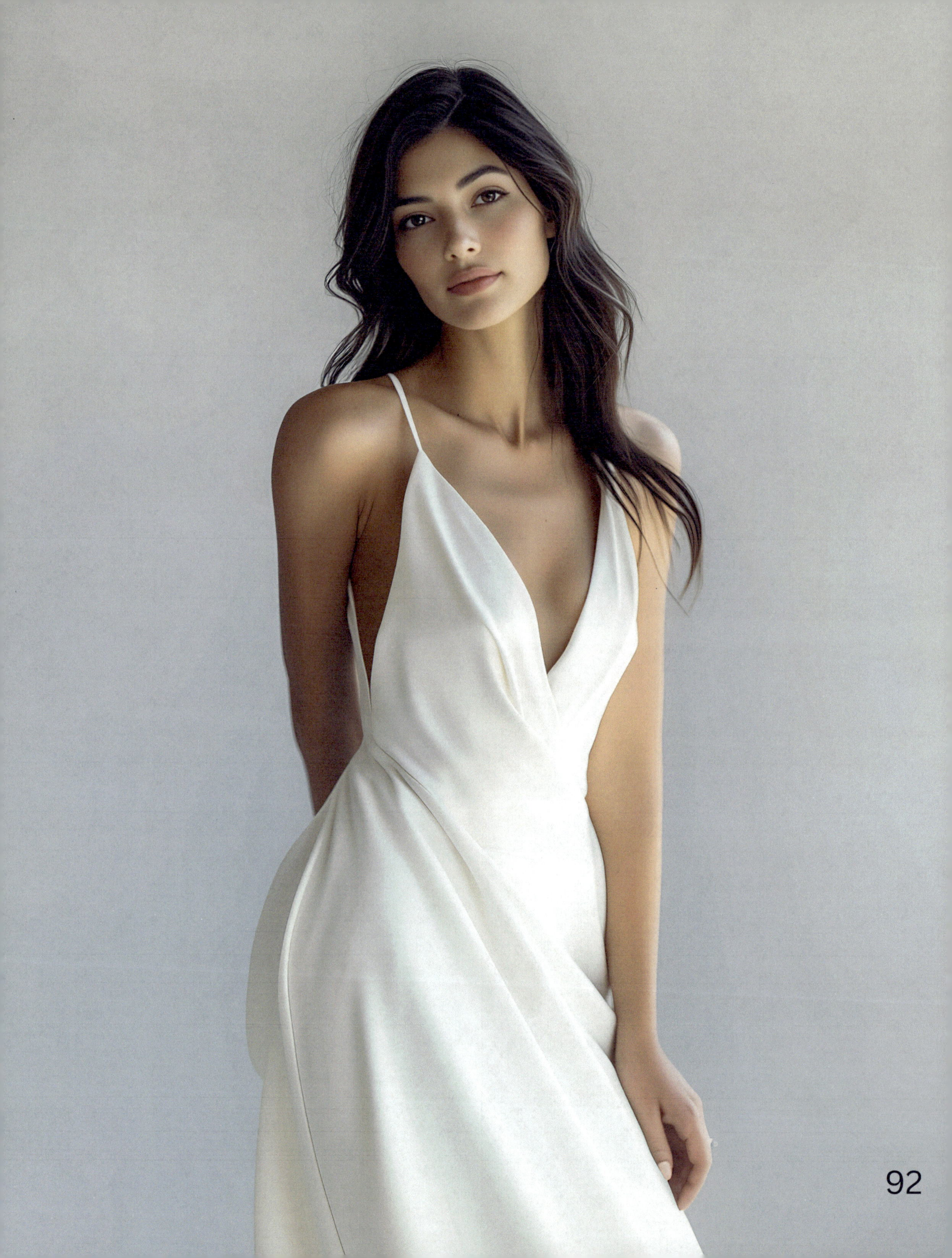

> *Minimalism in bridal fashion is more than just an aesthetic, but a philosophy that embraces elegance, sophistication, and the power of simplicity.*
>
> *A wedding dress does not need excessive embellishments to be breathtaking. Instead, it is the purity of design and the quality of craftsmanship.*

94

95

CHAPTER 4

EMBELLISHED MINIMALISM
When Details Make the Dress

―❝―――――

While minimalist wedding dresses are known for their clean lines and unembellished beauty, subtle detailing can enhance their elegance without overpowering the design. Beading, embroidery, and appliqué can all be incorporated in a way that feels intentional and refined, adding texture and depth while maintaining the minimalist aesthetic.

- *Delicate pearl accents.*
- *Hand-sewn embroidery that adds dimension without overwhelming the silhouette.*
- *Subtle sequin work that catches the light.*
- *Minimalist lace appliqués that blend seamlessly into the fabric for a soft, romantic effect.*

―――――❞―

97

VINTAGE REVERIE

— 66 ———————

Fashion has drawn inspiration from history, celebrating the elegance of the past while infusing it with modern sophistication, paying homage to iconic fashion moments, and proving that timeless style never fades. Each era has left its mark on bridal fashion.

The 1920s introduced bias-cut silk gowns, Art Deco embellishments, and flapper-inspired beading. The 1950s gave us the quintessential cinched-waist, full-skirt silhouette, made famous by legends like Audrey Hepburn and Grace Kelly. The drama of the Victorian and Baroque periods influenced corseted bodices, billowing skirts, and extravagant lace detailing, while the 1970s and 1980s embraced bohemian free-spiritedness and bold, voluminous sleeves.

——————— 99 —

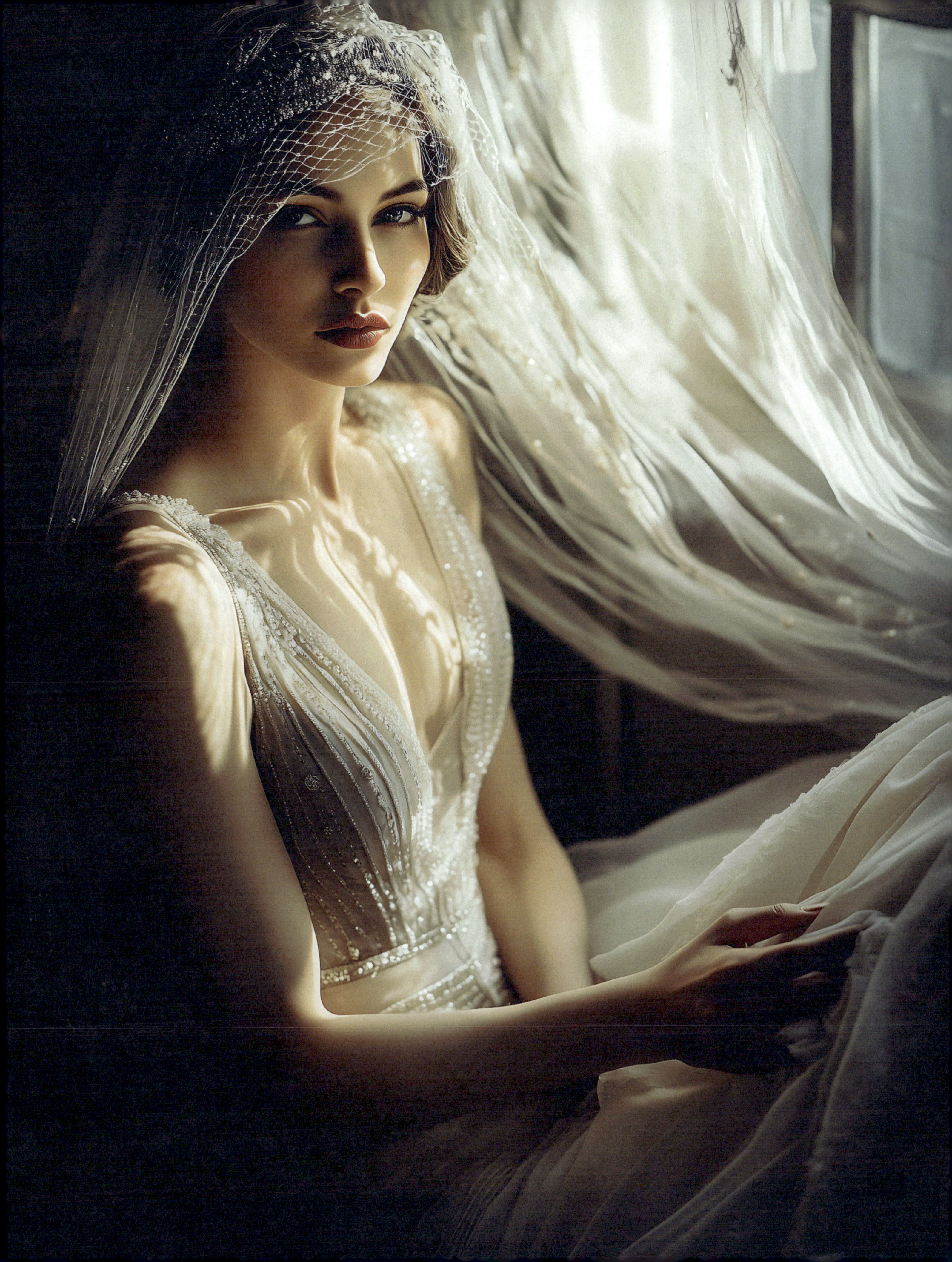

Timeless Couture Gowns Inspired by the Past

— 66 ———————

Vintage-inspired couture is about reinvention rather than replication. Modern designers take inspiration from these historical elements, reinterpreting them with contemporary fabrics, refined tailoring, and innovative techniques. A gown may feature hand-sewn lace reminiscent of the 19th century with a sleek, modern silhouette.

For the bride drawn to romance, nostalgia, and classic beauty, a vintage-inspired gown offers the best of both worlds: a connection to the past and a vision of timeless elegance for the future. These gowns remind us that while trends may come and go, grace, refinement, and artistry endure forever.

——————— 99 —

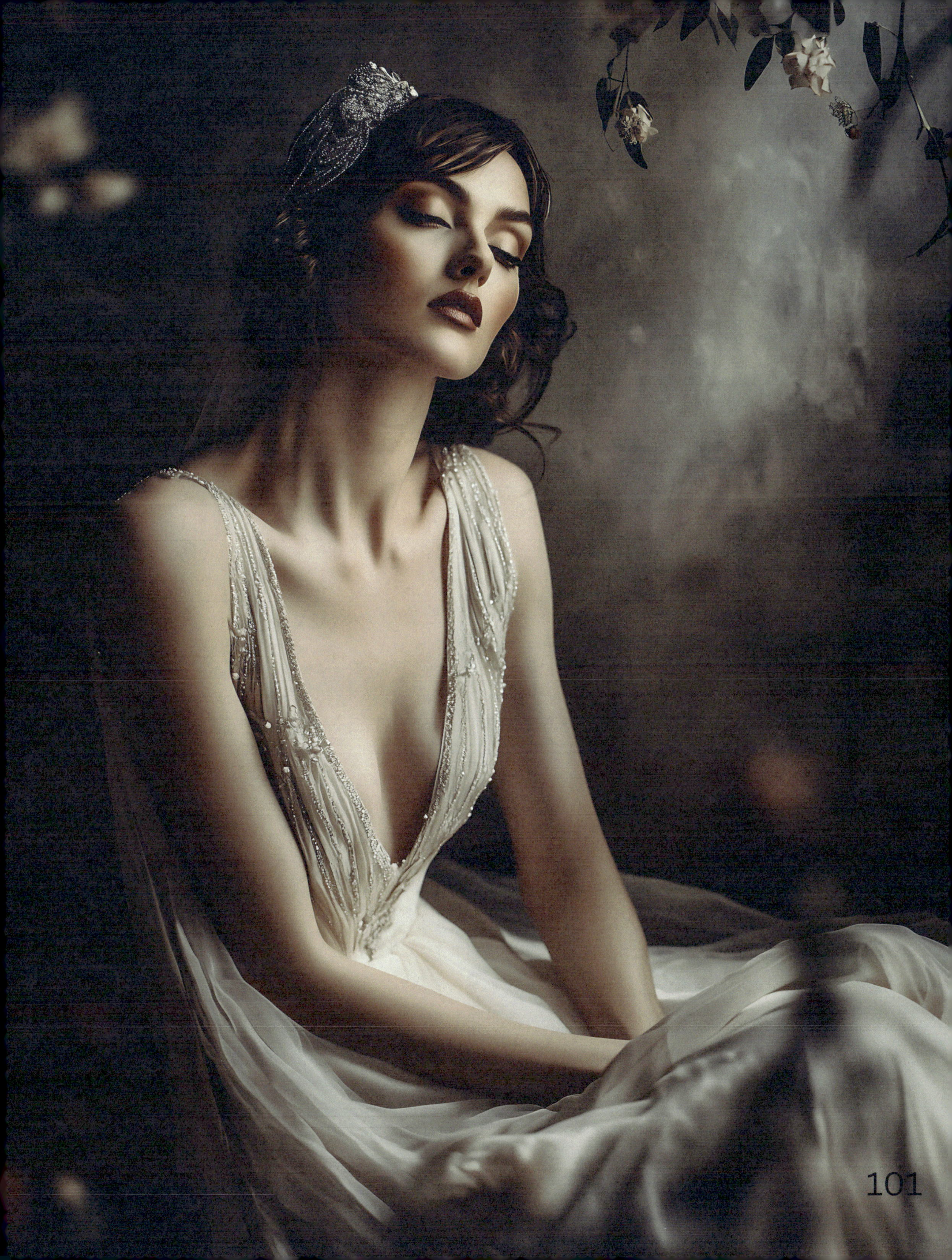

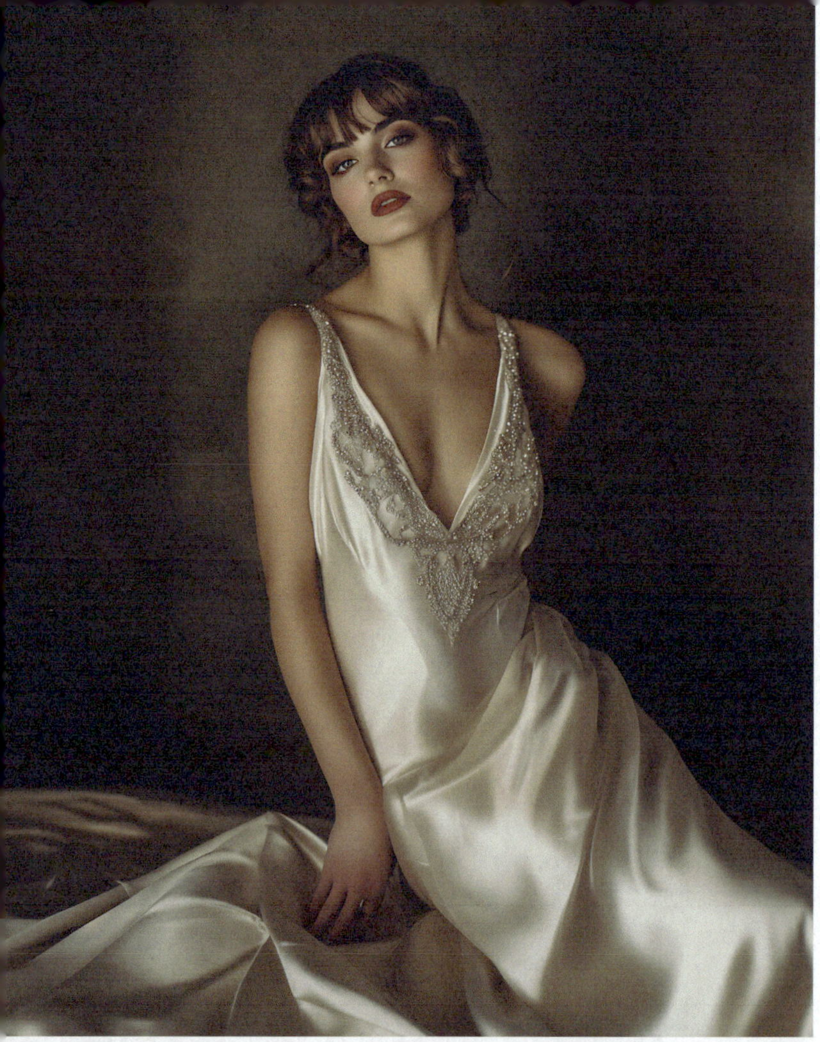

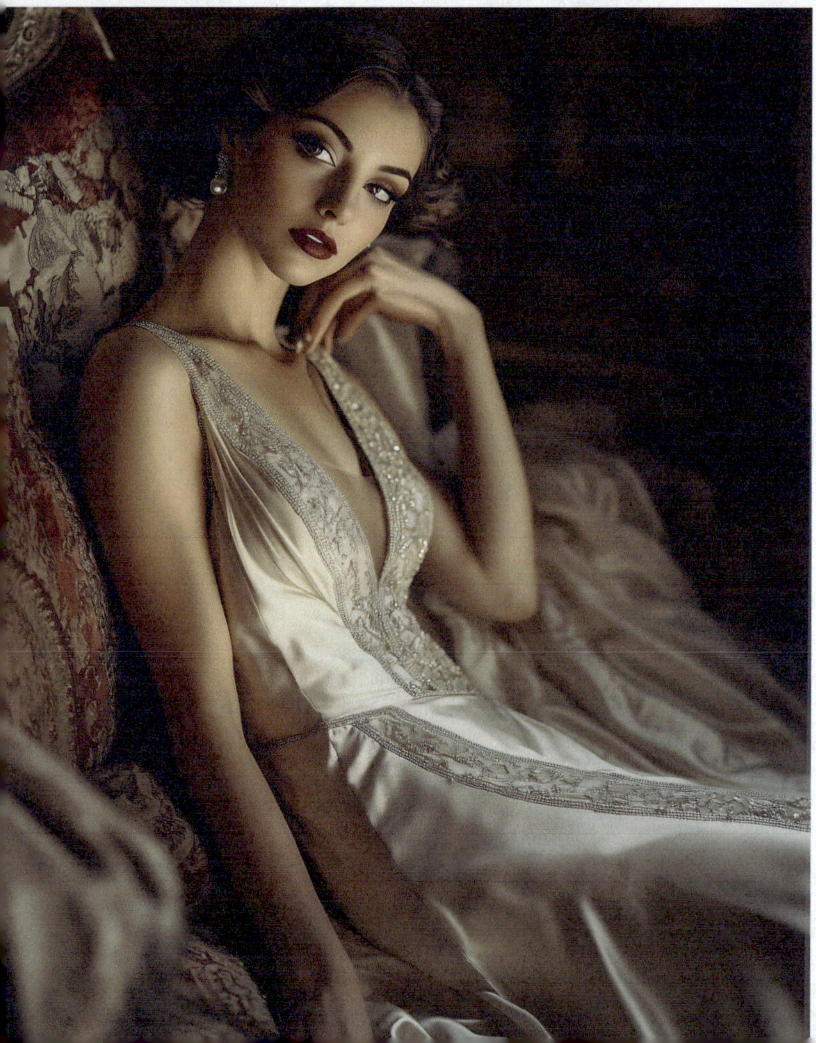

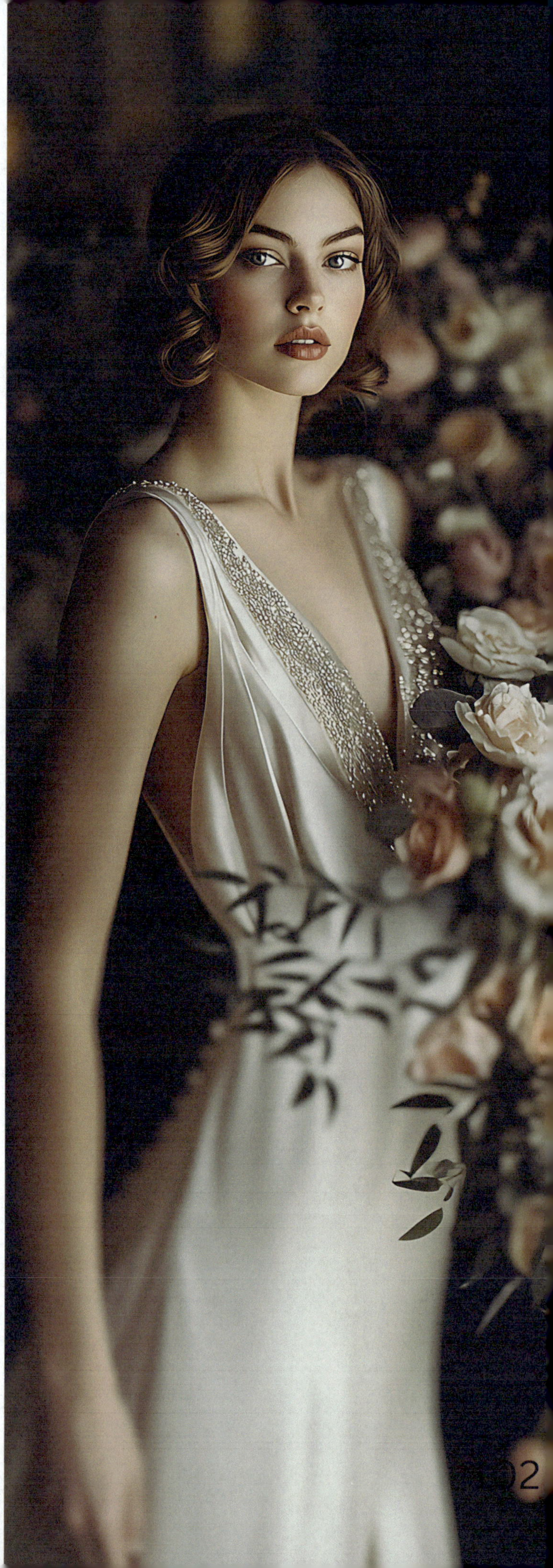

THE ERA OF GLAMOUR AND FREEDOM

> *The 1920s marked a dramatic shift in fashion, including bridal couture. As society embraced a more modern, liberated lifestyle, wedding gowns reflected this change with fluid silhouettes, luxurious fabrics, and intricate embellishments. Gone were the restrictive corsets and heavy layers of past eras. The 1920s couture wedding gowns exuded effortless elegance and movement.*

104

105

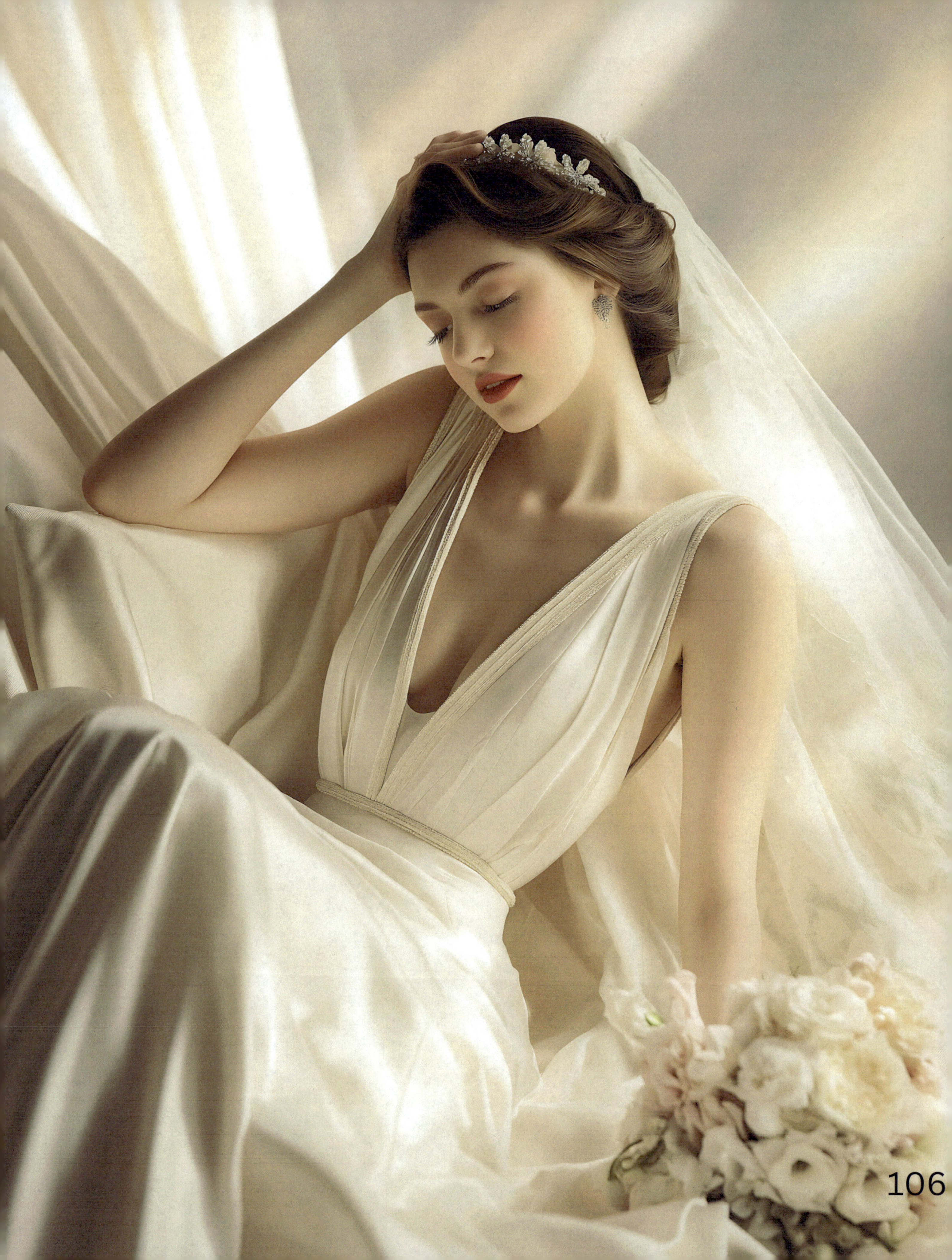

> Used sparingly and with purpose, embellishments can transform a gown into something truly special.

Art Deco Elegance

— 66 ⎯⎯⎯⎯⎯⎯

The Art Deco era of the 1920s and 1930s was a period of bold glamour, geometric precision, and modern sophistication. Wedding gowns from this time reflected the luxury and opulence of the Jazz Age, combining sleek silhouettes with intricate embellishments that embodied the spirit of progress and innovation.

Unlike the voluminous gowns of previous eras, Art Deco bridal couture embraced streamlined, column-like silhouettes, often featuring drop waists, delicate cap sleeves, and flowing trains. Luxurious fabrics like silk satin, charmeuse, and chiffon gave these gowns an effortlessly elegant drape, while elaborate hand-beaded embellishments added shimmering decadence.

⎯⎯⎯⎯⎯⎯ 99 —

109

Intricate geometric beadwork, metallic embroidery, and symmetrical patterns were defining elements of this era, inspired by the sleek lines of architecture, fine jewelry, and the excitement of the Roaring Twenties. Designers constructed gowns with beaded fringes, scalloped edges, and artful appliqués, creating a dazzling interplay of light and movement.

Veils were often long and sheer, cascading elegantly from ornate headpieces or Juliet caps adorned with pearls and crystals. Brides also favored embellished gloves, statement earrings, and T-strap heels for an effortlessly chic look.

111

112

> The Art Deco wedding gown remains a timeless symbol of vintage glamour and refined sophistication.
>
> For brides drawn to the elegance of Old Hollywood, the allure of Gatsby-era luxury, or the precision of geometric beauty, an Art Deco-inspired gown offers a stunning tribute to one of fashion's most dazzling periods.

ELEGANT EMBROIDERY

Minimalism with a Delicate Touch

> *Minimalist wedding dresses embrace simplicity, but that doesn't mean they lack detail. When used thoughtfully, embroidery can add depth, texture, and artistry while maintaining a refined and timeless aesthetic. Whether it's delicate floral motifs, subtle geometric patterns, or fine threadwork that shimmers in the light, minimalist embroidery enhances a gown without overwhelming its sleek silhouette.*
>
> *These dresses embody the perfect balance between simplicity and detail, each stitch carefully placed to complement, rather than overshadow, the purity of design. These gowns prove that slight embellishments can create a stunning, unforgettable effect, elevating minimalism into something truly exquisite.*

115

116

117

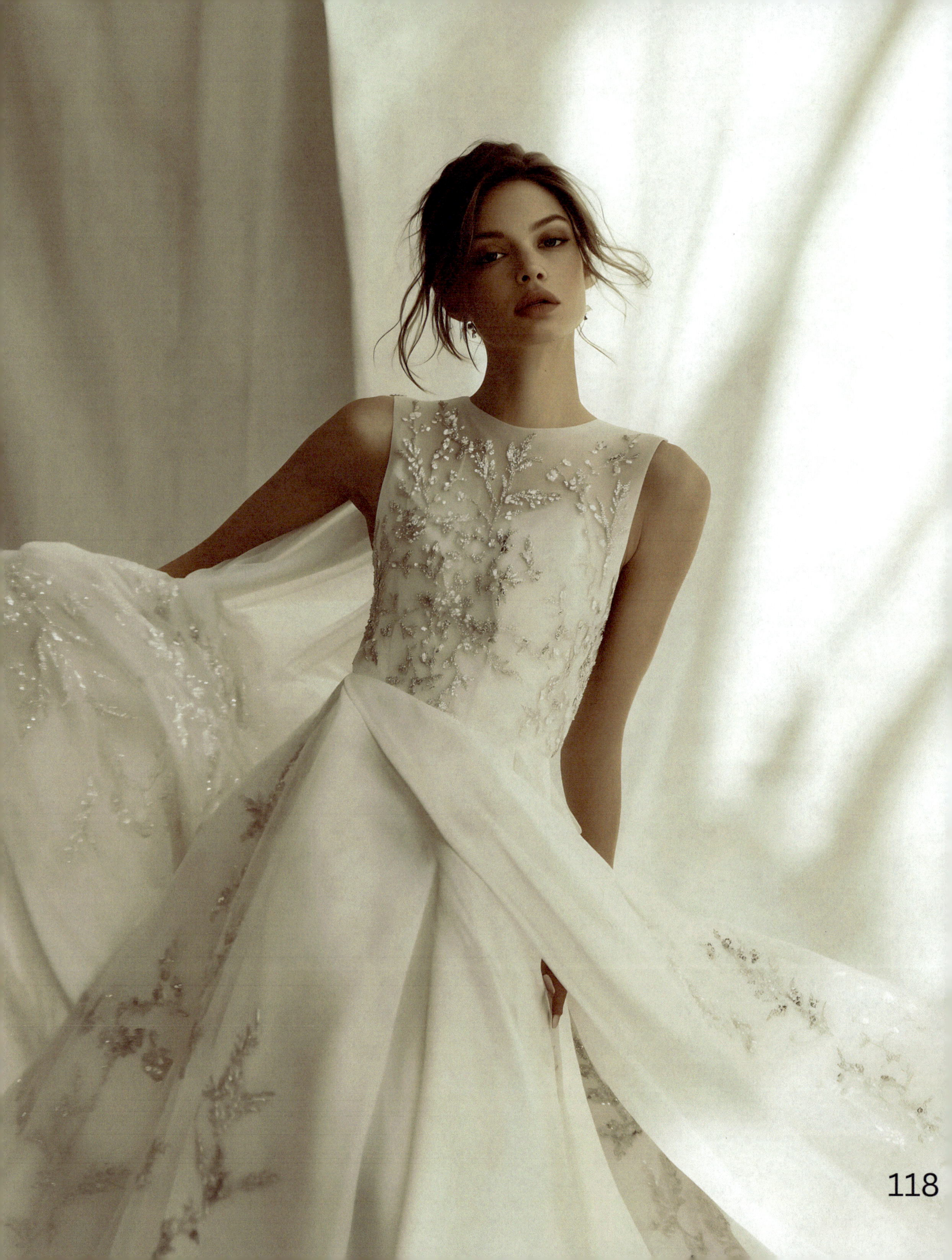

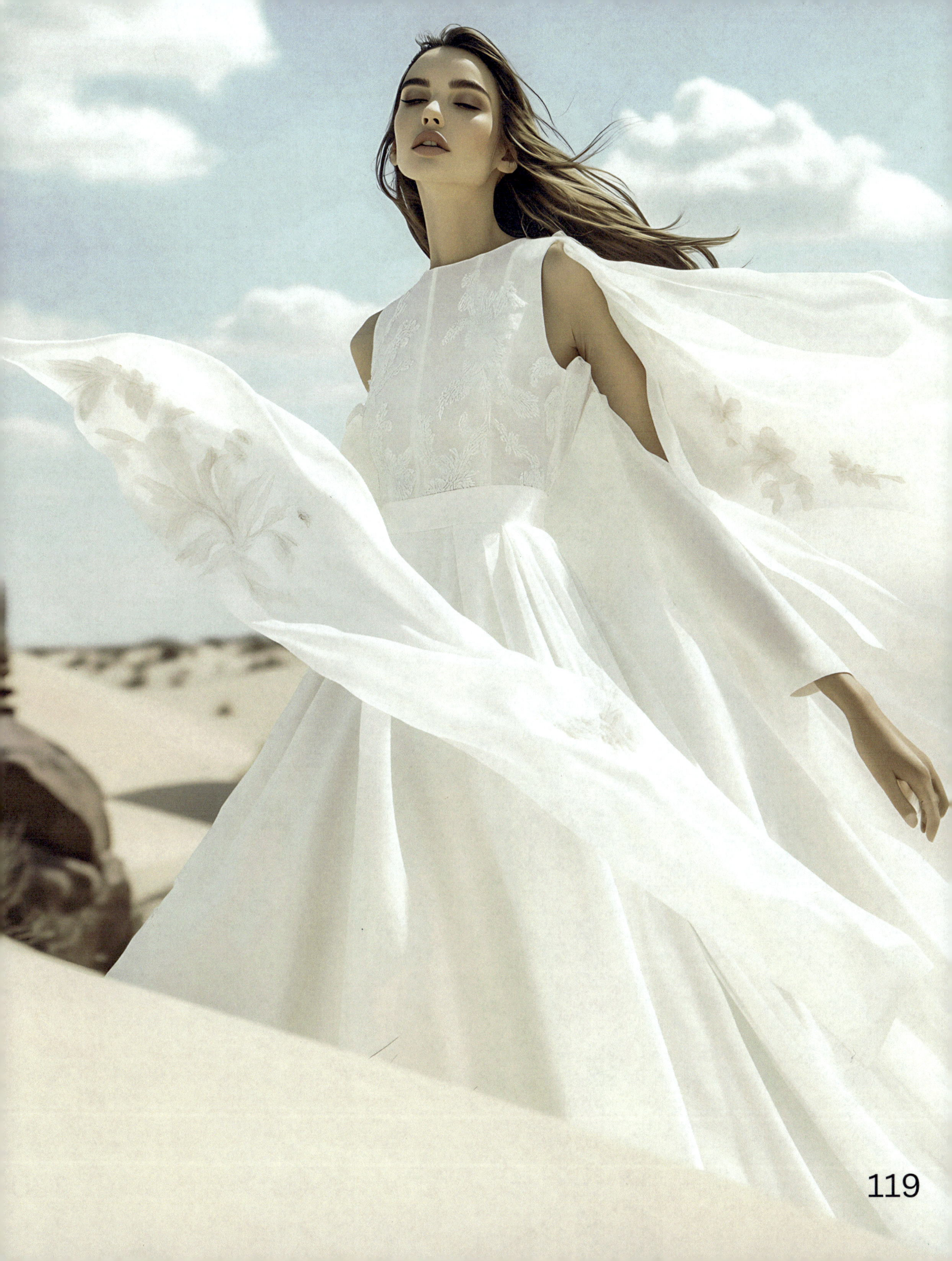

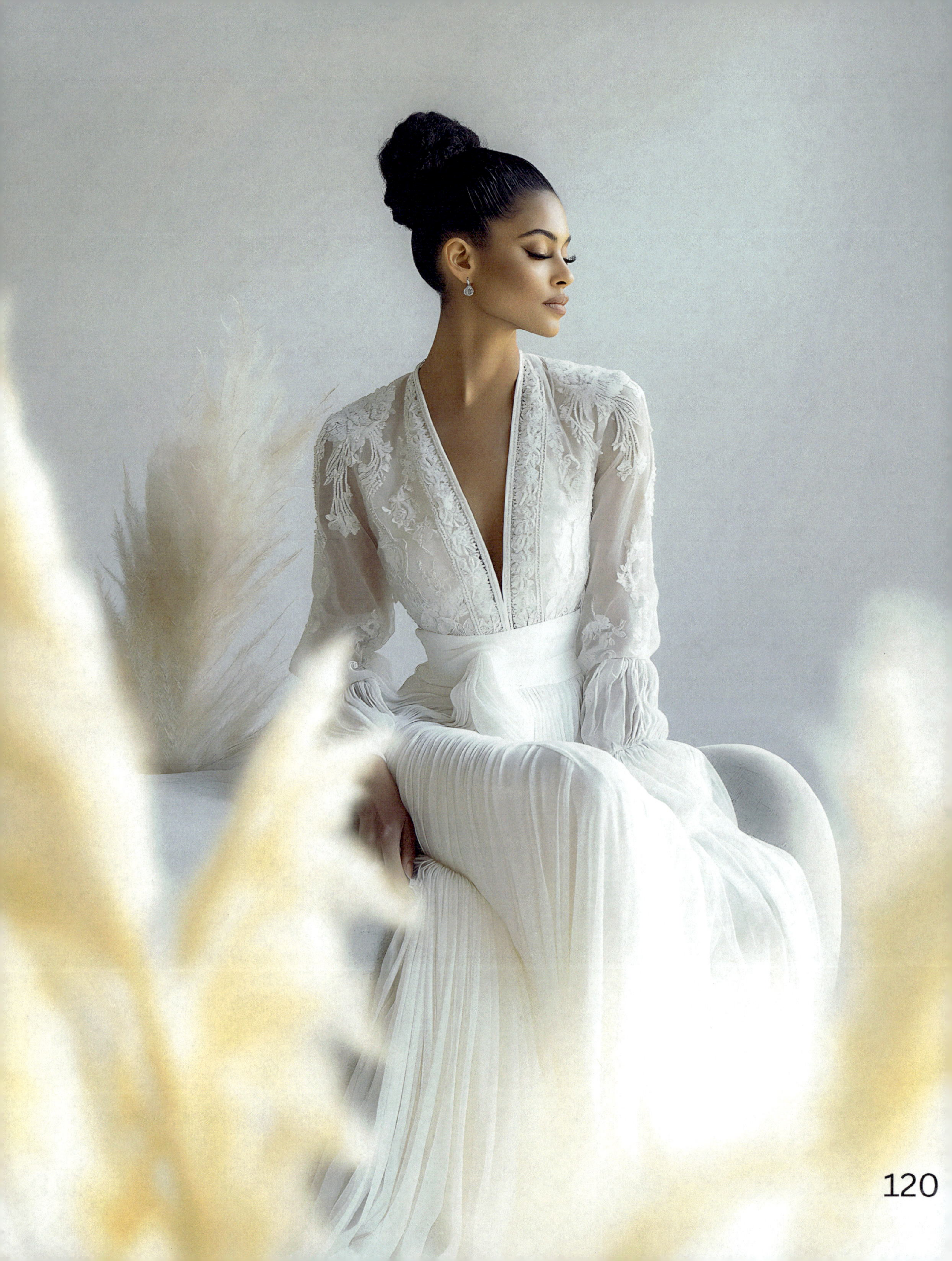

121

122

123

The Allure of Romantic Couture

— 66 ——

The details are intricate yet subtle, with motifs that mimic vines and blossoms, pearl-threaded embroidery that catches the light, and barely-there beading. These gowns are not about excess but deliberate softness, evoking the beauty of romanticism and nature.

—————— 99 —

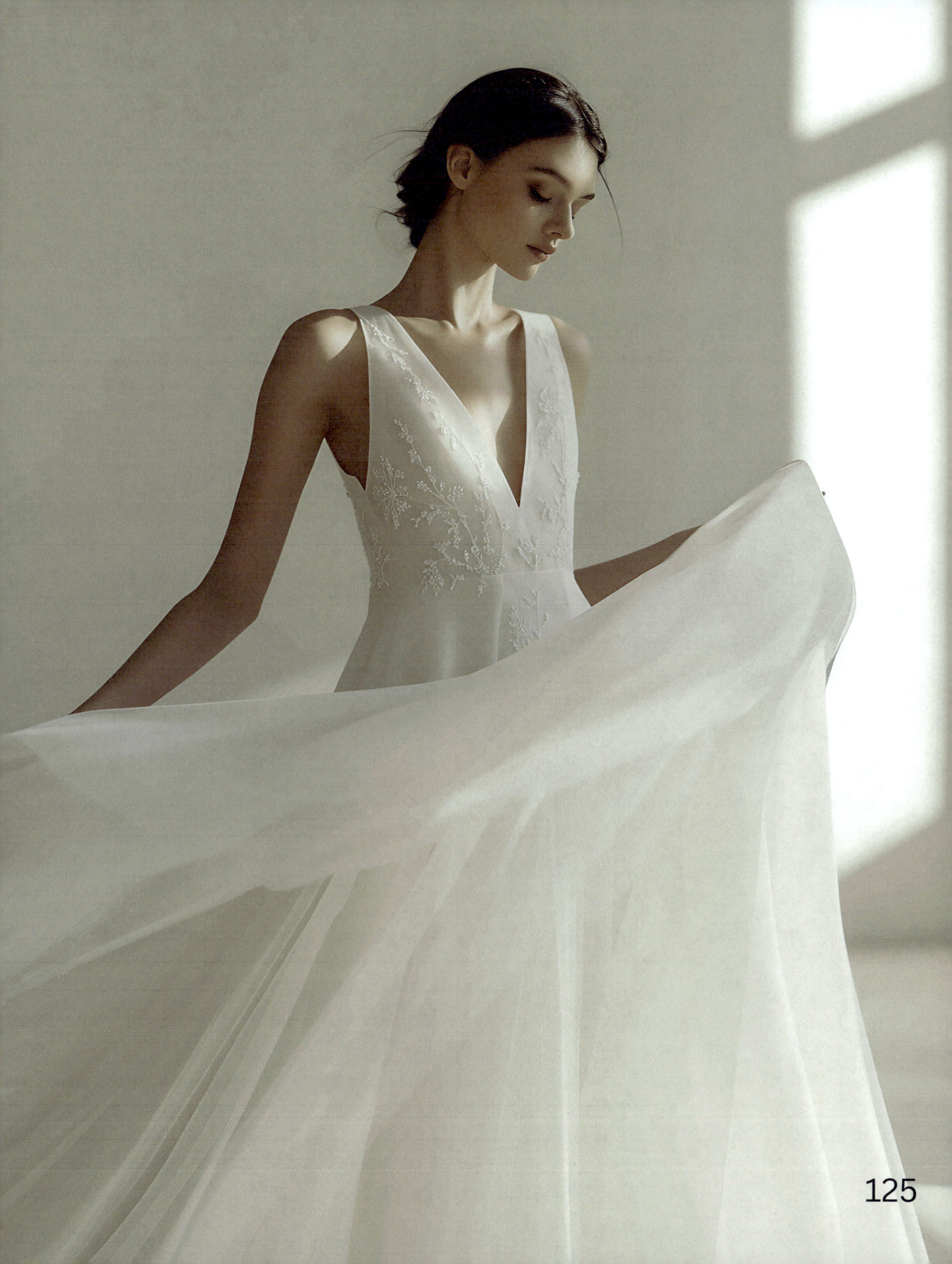

126

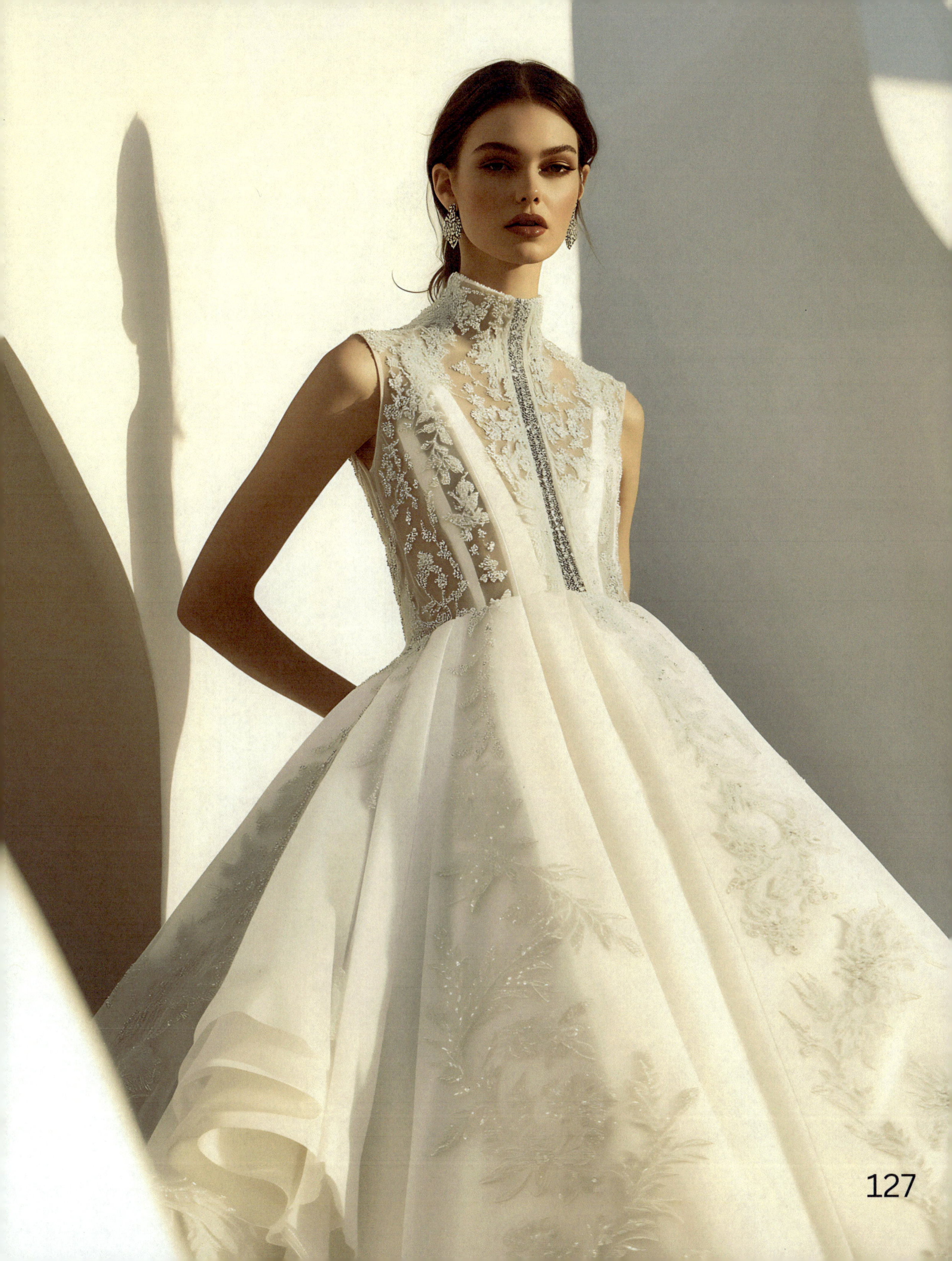

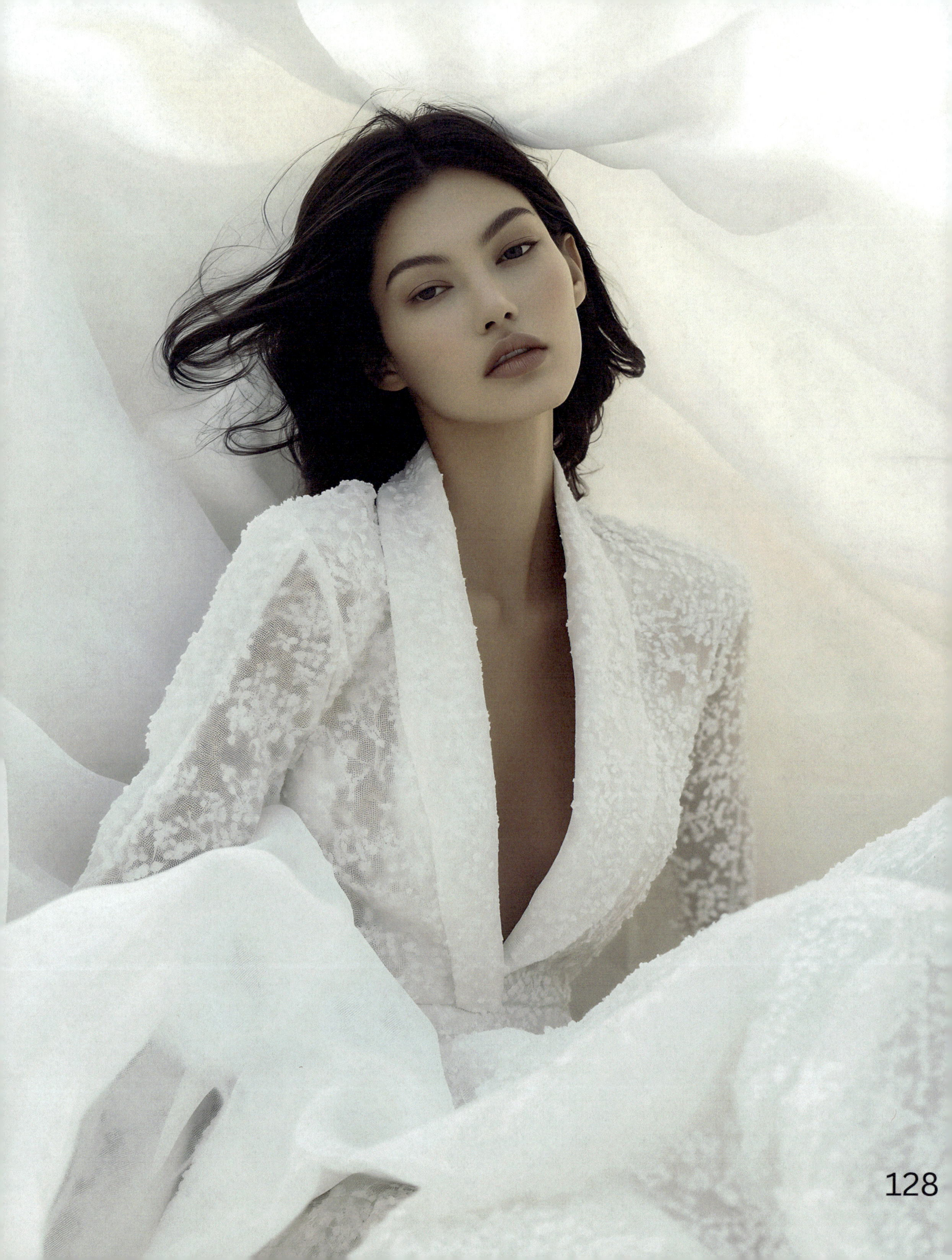

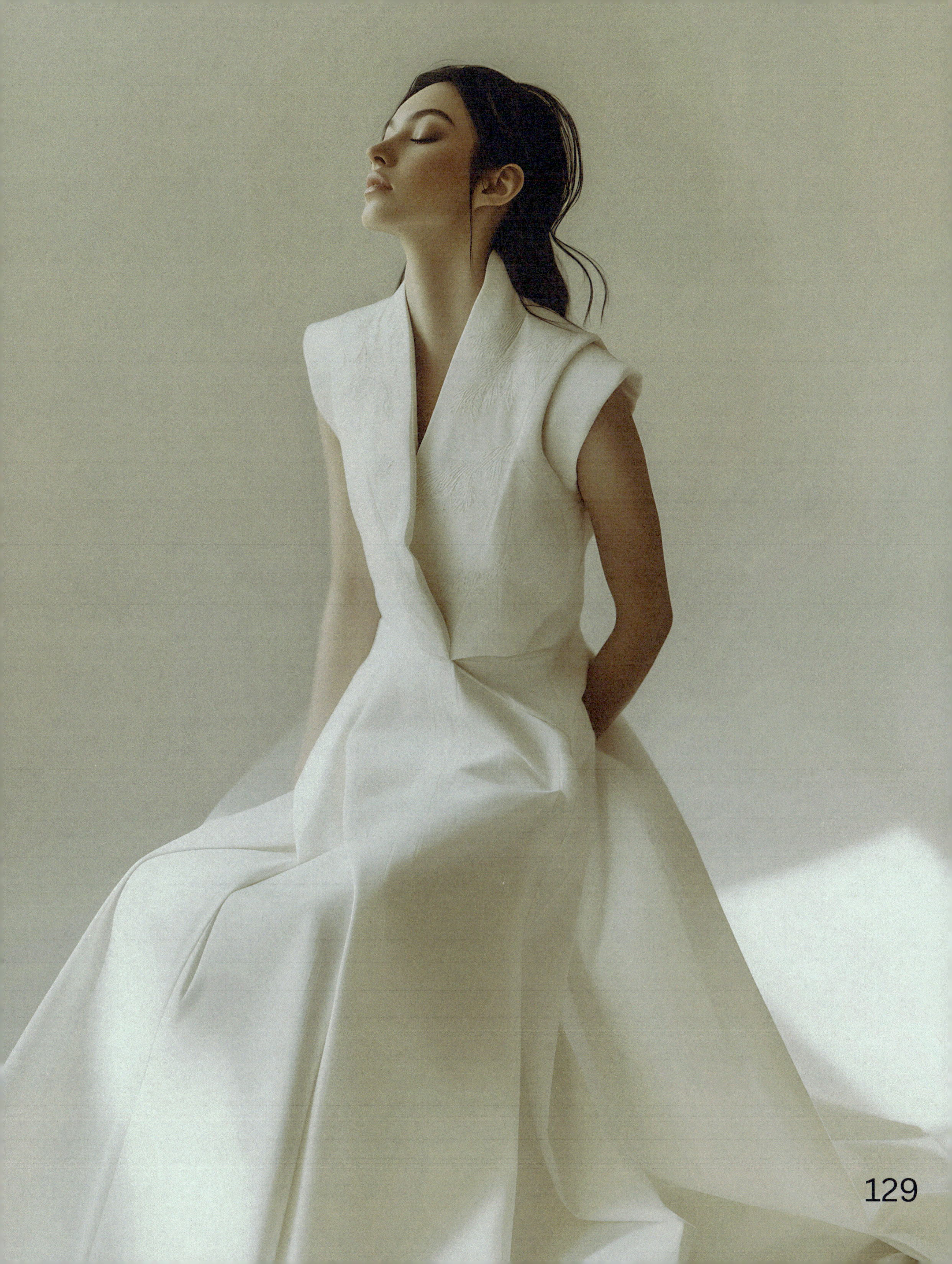

CHAPTER 5

MODERN LACE

A Minimalist Approach to a Classic Fabric

— 66 ——————

Lace is one of the most beloved fabrics in bridal fashion. It takes on a fresh and modern approach with minimalist designs. Rather than ornate patterns and heavy embroidery, modern lace is delicate, sheer, and thoughtfully placed to enhance the silhouette rather than overwhelm it.

This chapter explores how lace can be used in minimalist wedding dresses, adding structure without excess. For brides who love the romance of lace but prefer a cleaner, more modern interpretation, this chapter showcases gowns that balance tradition with a fresh, refined look.

—————————— 66 —

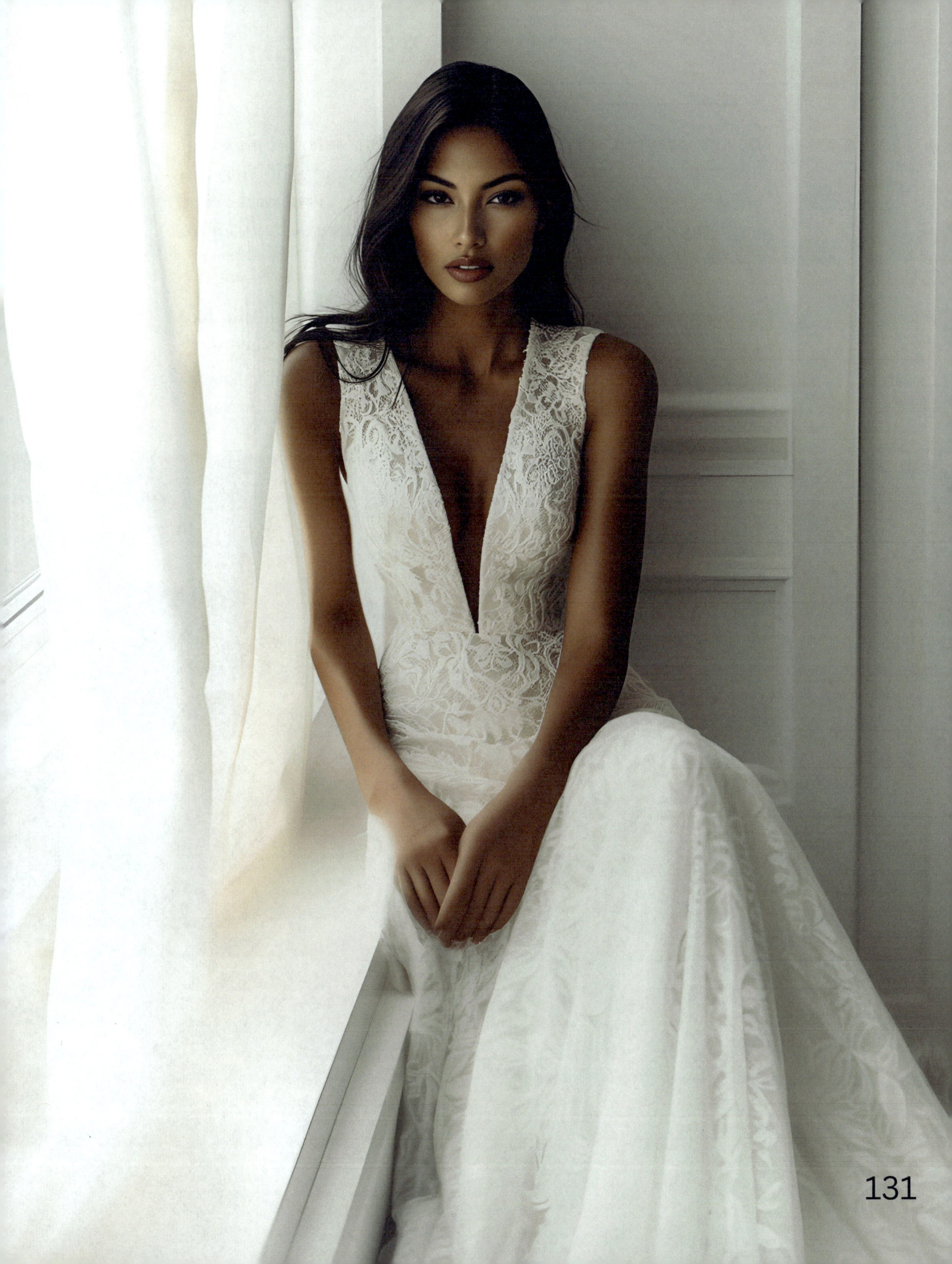

> *Designers often draw inspiration from the ethereal muses of history and legend, such as the soft drapery of Grecian goddesses, the effortless elegance of Pre-Raphaelite paintings, and the flowing silhouettes showcased in haute couture runway collections.*
>
> *Sleeves might be sheer and billowy, skirts cascading like waterfalls, and bodices adorned with delicate embroidery that tells a story of love and artistry.*

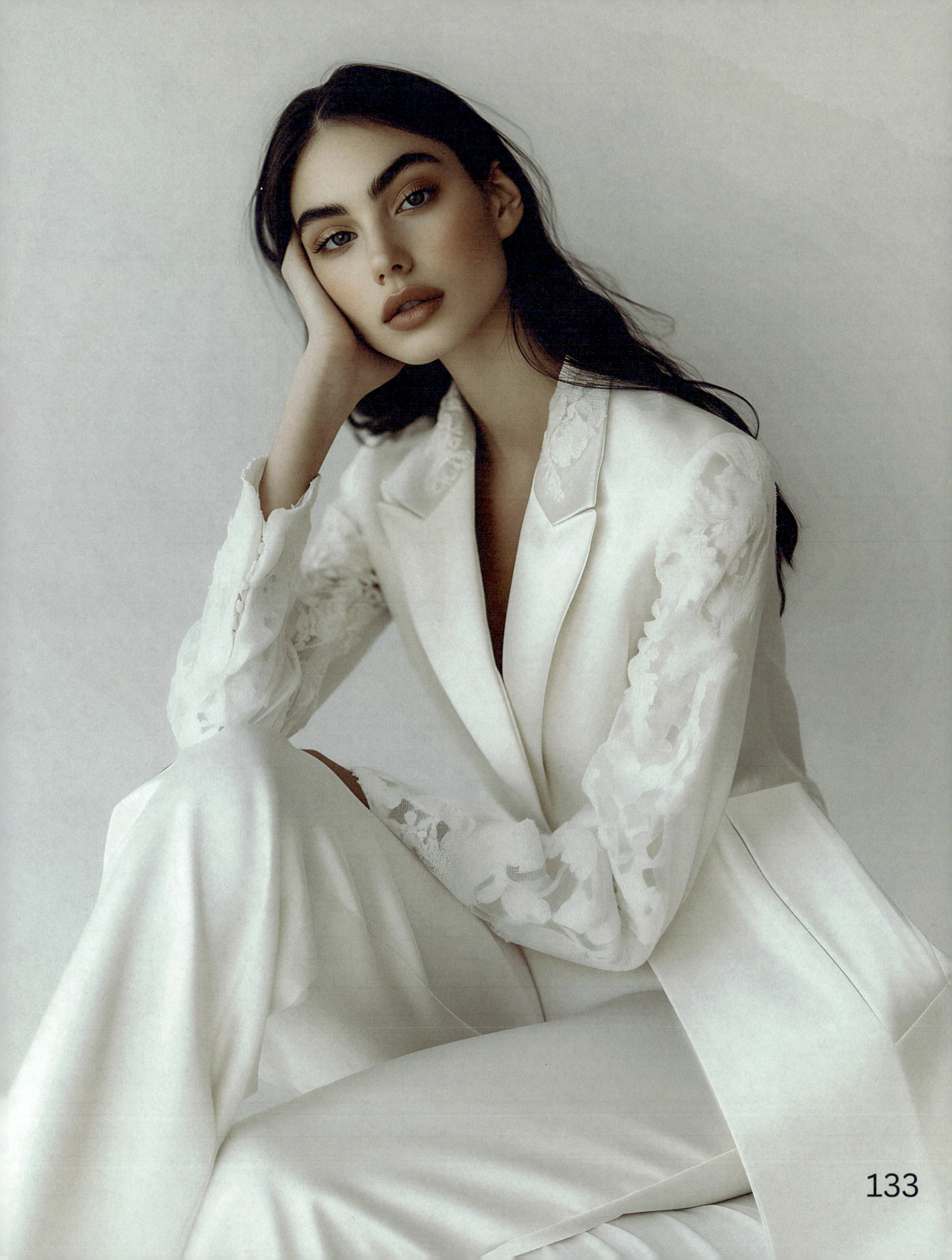

134

135

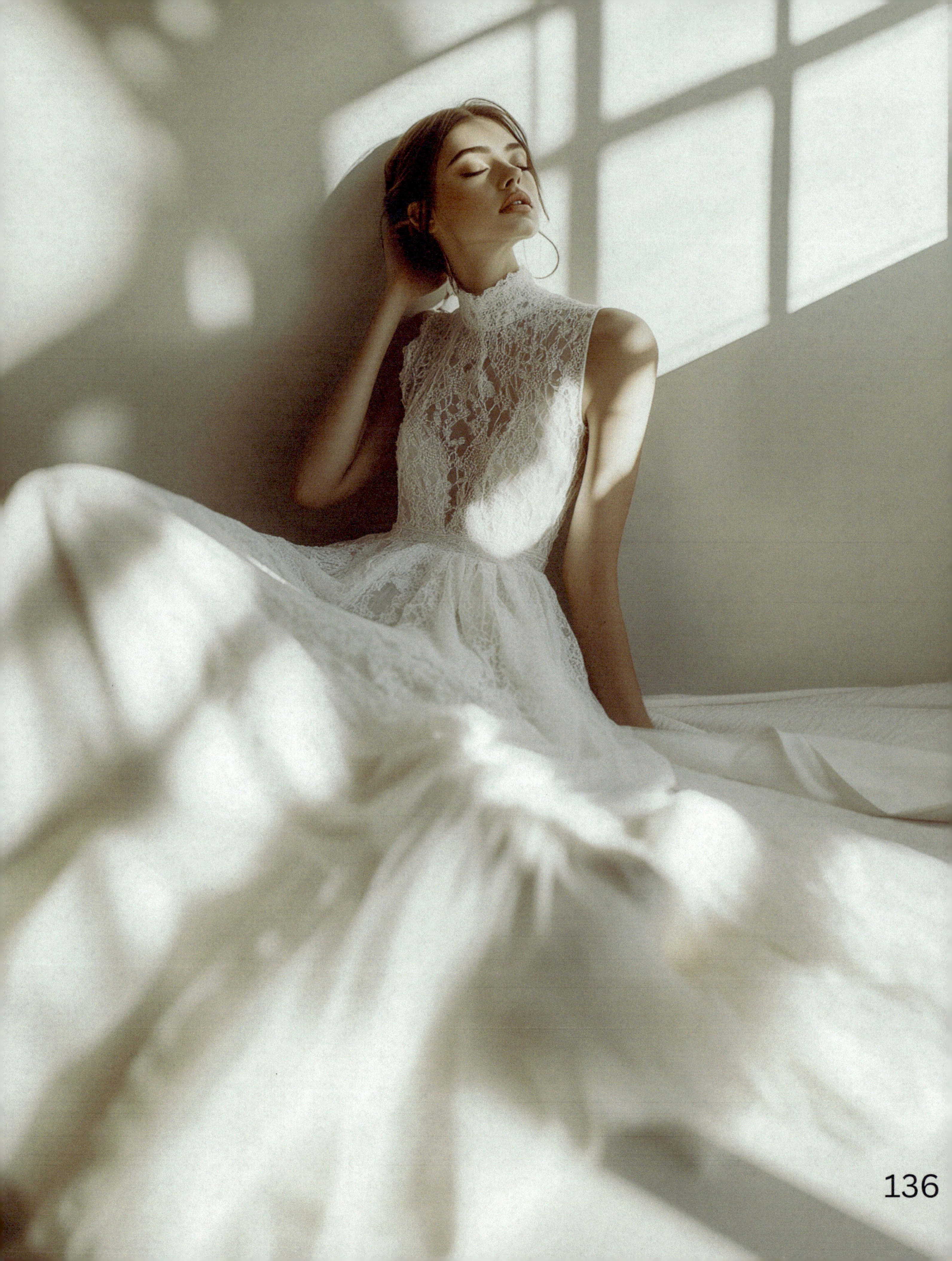

137

138

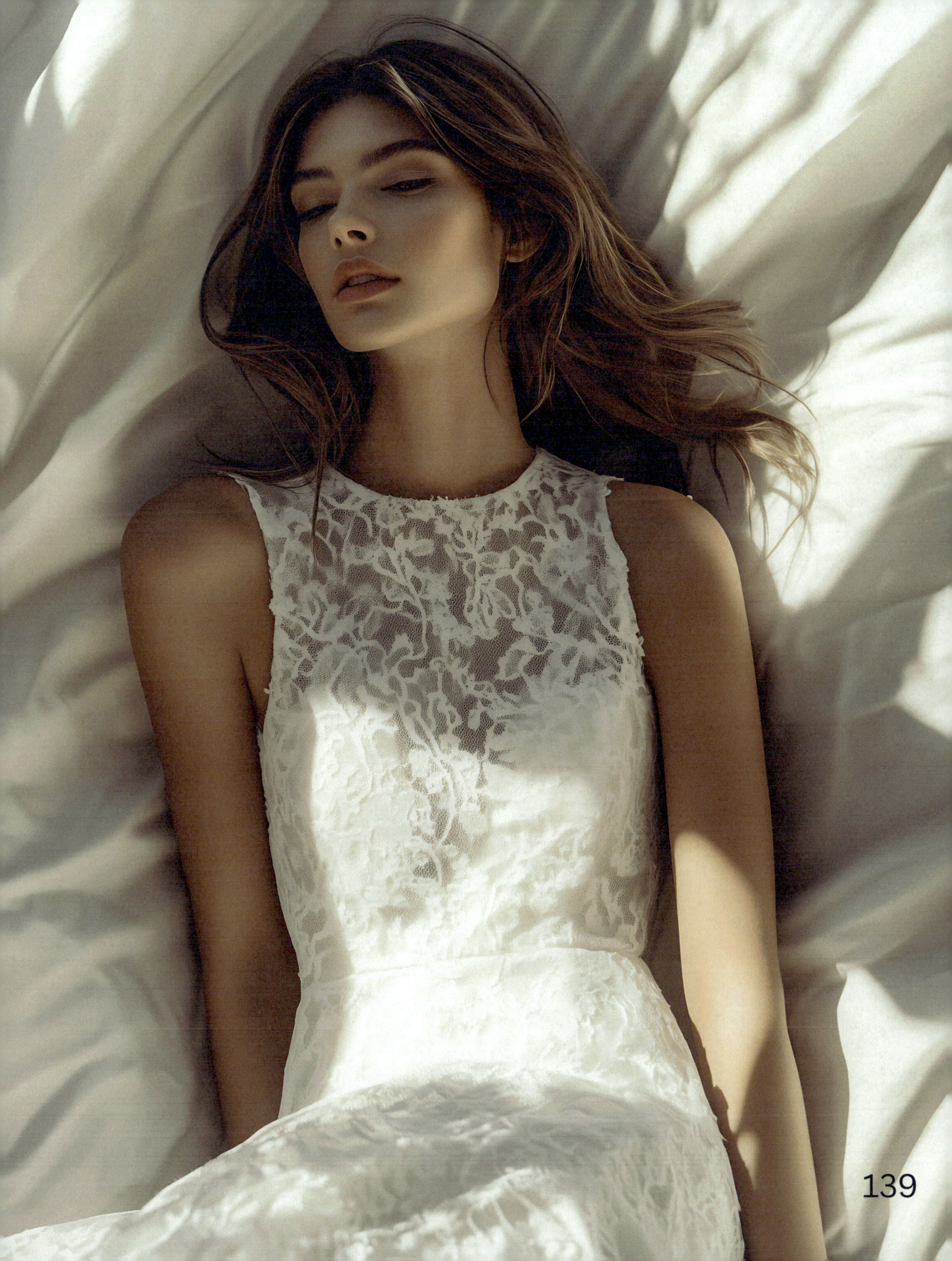

140

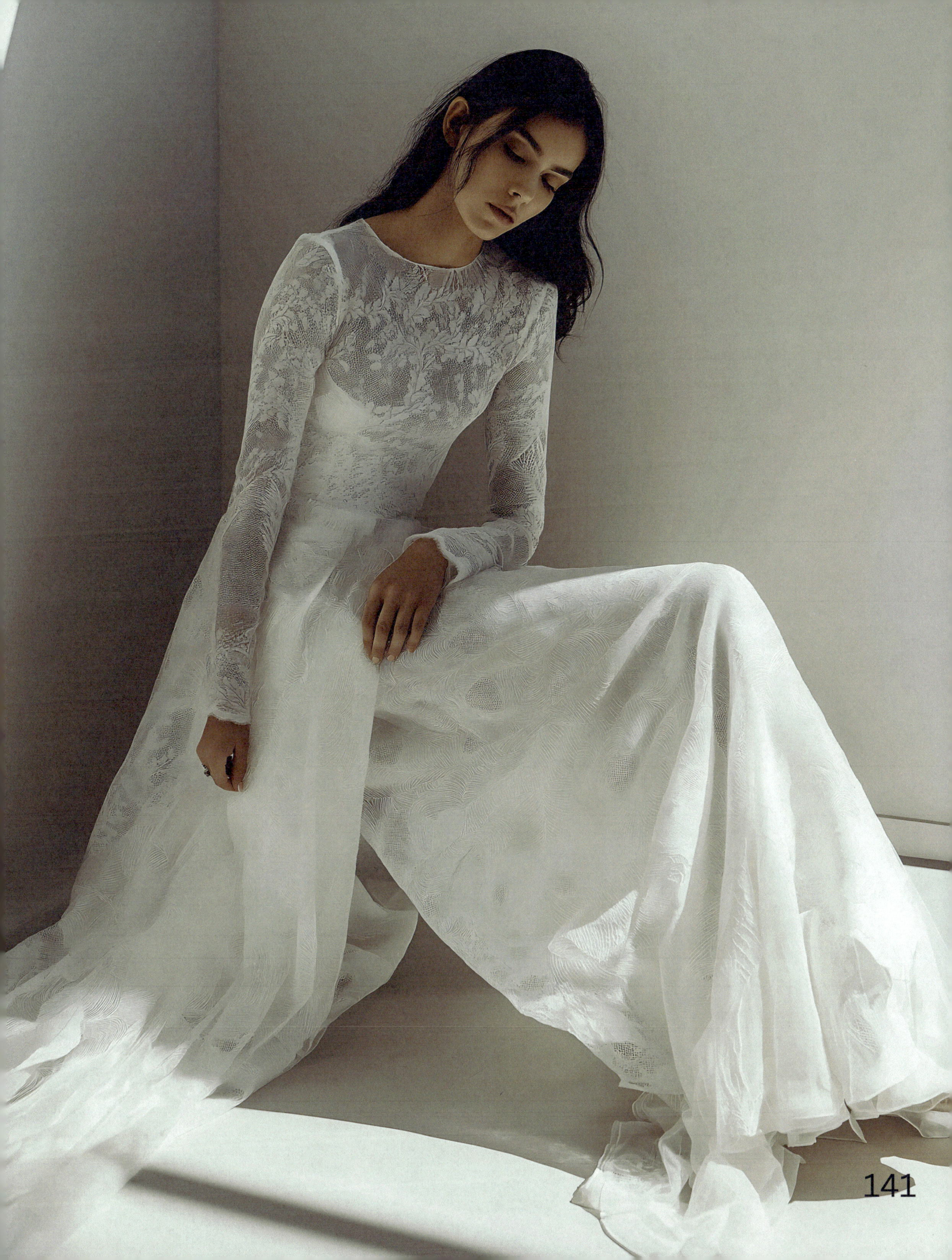

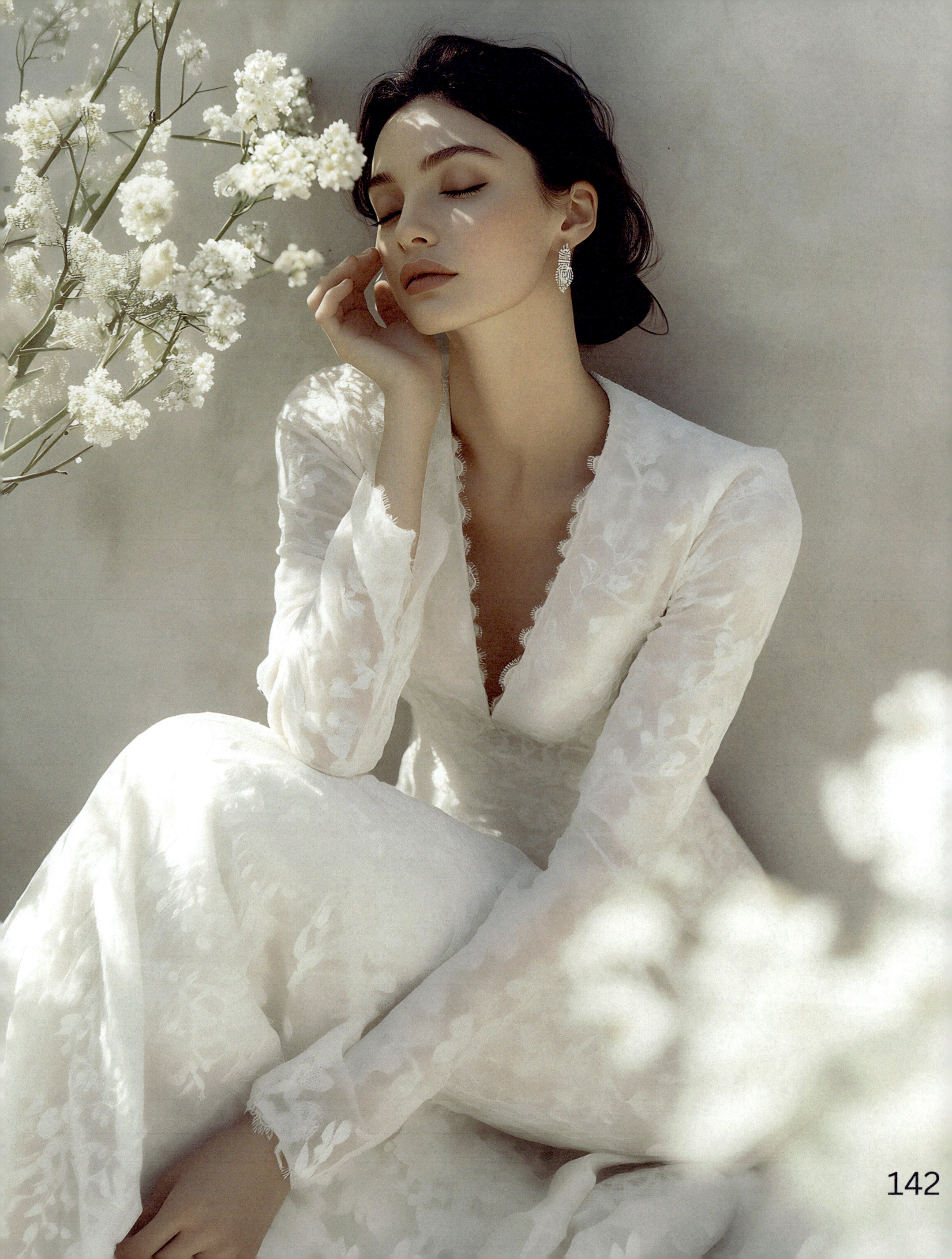

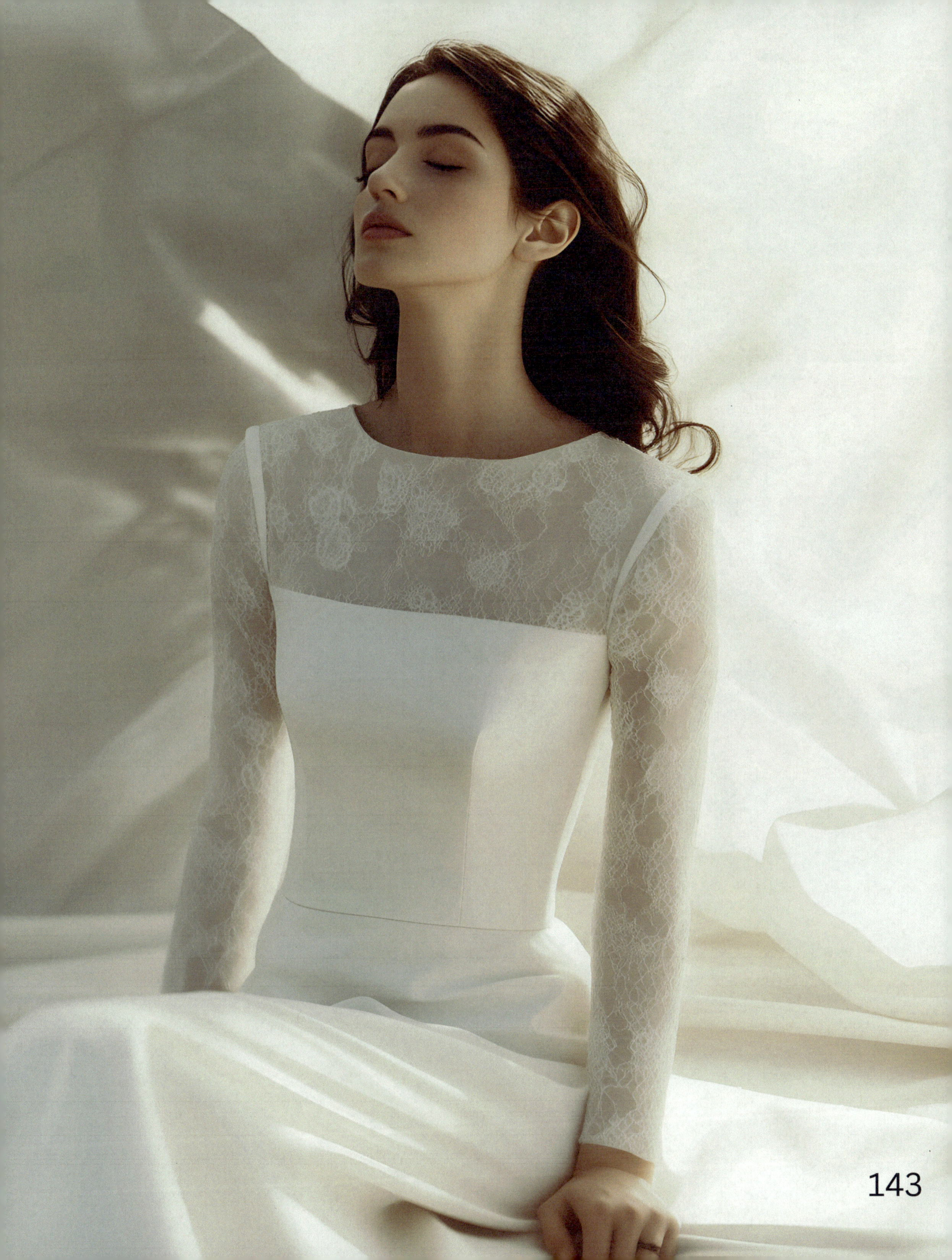

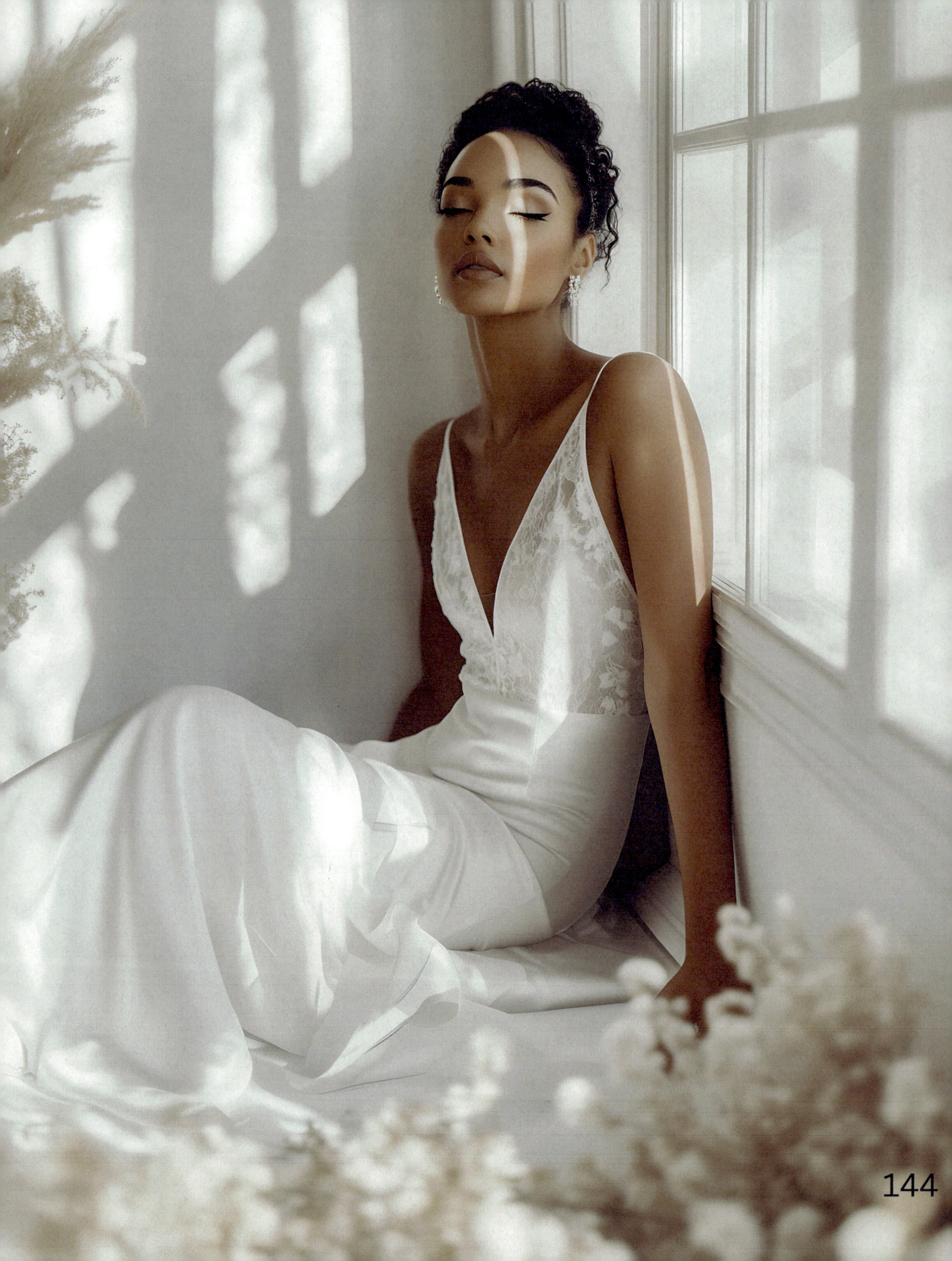

CONCLUSION

The Enduring Beauty of Minimalism

— 66 ⎯⎯⎯⎯⎯⎯⎯

We have explored the many facets of minimalist wedding dresses. From sleek silhouettes to subtle detailing, modern lace interpretations, and a refined use of texture. Each gown tells a story of restraint and refinement, proving that a bride does not need extravagance to make a lasting impression.

For the modern bride who values timeless style, a minimalist wedding dress offers something far more meaningful than fleeting trends. Whether it is a crisp satin sheath, a delicately structured A-line, or a gown with a unique yet understated twist, these dresses celebrate the art of less is more, an aesthetic that will remain effortlessly chic for years to come.

As you embark on your journey to find the perfect wedding dress, let this collection inspire you to embrace the beauty of simplicity. Whether you prefer the clean lines of a contemporary gown or the delicate charm of a subtly embellished dress, remember that the most stunning bridal look is the one that feels like you.

The perfect wedding dress is not just about fashion but how it makes you feel as you step into a new chapter of your life. Radiant in the confidence that comes from knowing you have chosen something timeless.

⎯⎯⎯⎯⎯⎯⎯ 99 —

Made in United States
Troutdale, OR
04/08/2025